Oxford Picture Dictionary of American English

English/Spanish Edition

E. C. PARNWELL

ILLUSTRATED BY
BERNARD CASE
CORINNE CLARKE
RAY BURROWS

SPANISH LINGUISTIC CONSULTANTS
MIGDALIA ROMERO DE ORTIZ
EFRAÍN BARRERA
EDUARDO ORDOÑEZ
RICARDO OTHEGUY

New York   OXFORD UNIVERSITY PRESS

Oxford University Press

200 Madison Avenue
New York, NY 10016 USA

Walton Street
Oxford OX2 6DP England

OXFORD is a trademark of Oxford University Press.

Library of Congress Cataloging-in-Publication Data

Parnwell, E.C.
Oxford picture dictionary of American English.
Includes index.
SUMMARY: Teaches English as a second language to
Spanish speakers through the use of pictures dealing
with everyday topics such as the body, post office,
law, travel, and family.
1. English language in the United States.
2. Picture dictionaries, English. 3. English language
—Text-books for foreigners—Spanish. [1. English
language—Text-books for foreigners—Spanish.] I. Case,
Bernard. II. Clarke, Corrine. III. Burrows, Ray.
IV. Title.
PE2835.5.P37   423   77-18464
ISBN 0-19-502333-1

Notes from the English Language Teaching Department

We are proud to present the first contextualized Oxford Picture Dictionary
using American English. This dictionary can be used for communicative
purposes. It will stimulate exciting conversations about everyday topics
which students come in contact with. It can also be used as a handy
reference for students studying on their own.

We have made every possible attempt to include the major lexical regional
variants in the Spanish text.

We hope you enjoy using this dictionary. We welcome your comments as
always.

Una nota del departamento de Inglés

Estamos muy orgullosos de poder presentarles el primer diccionario ilustrado
y contextualizado usando el Inglés Americano.

Se puede usar este diccionario con el propósito de enriquecer la
comunicación oral. Además servirá como estímulo para conversaciones de
temas comunes los cuales los estudiantes enfrentan diariamente. También se
puede usar como ayuda para los estudiantes que prefieren estudiar
individualmente.

Hemos hecho el mayor esfuerzo para incluir en el texto Español las
variaciones regionales mas importantes de cada palabra.

Esperamos que el lector disfrute del uso de este diccionario. Como siempre
nos gustaría saber sus opiniones y sugerencias al respecto.

Printing: 20 19 18 17 16
Printed in Hong Kong.

CONTENTS / INDICE

Nuestro Universo	**4**	Our Universe
El Mundo	**5**	The World
El Cuerpo Humano	**8**	The Human Body
La Vestimenta/La Ropa	**10**	Clothes
En la Ciudad	**14**	In the City
La Ley	**16**	The Law
Los Servicios Médicos y de Incendios	**17**	Fire and Medical Services
La Educación	**18**	Education
En el Supermercado	**20**	In the Supermarket
En la Oficina	**21**	In the Office
En el Correo	**22**	At the Post Office
En una Construcción/Una Obra	**23**	On a Building Site
En un Taller	**24**	In a Workshop
Las Herramientas	**25**	Tools
Una Casa	**26**	A House
El Tiempo/En el Patio	**27**	The Weather/The Yard
El Vestíbulo/El Pasillo	**28**	The Hall
La Sala	**29**	The Living Room
La Cocina	**30**	The Kitchen
Los Artículos del Hogar	**31**	Household Objects
El Dormitorio/La Recámara/El Bebé	**32**	The Bedroom/The Baby
El Cuarto de Baño	**33**	The Bathroom
En el Campo	**34**	In the Country
Acampar y En la Playa	**35**	Camping and the Seaside
En la Finca/En la Granja	**36**	On the Farm
La Fuerza Eléctrica/La Energía Eléctrica	**37**	Power
Los Viajes	**38**	Travel
Las Fuerzas Armadas	**45**	National Defense
La Recreacíon	**46**	Recreation
La Costura	**53**	Sewing
Las Ocupaciones/Las Profesiones	**54**	Occupations/Professions
Los Animales	**56**	Animals
Las Plantas	**61**	Plants
Los Verbos	**64**	Verbs
Los Recipientes/Los Envases	**67**	Containers
La Geometría	**68**	Lines and Shapes
Las Medidas	**69**	Measurement
La Hora, La Fecha, La Temperatura	**70**	Time, Date, Temperature
Las Relaciones Familiares	**71**	Family Relationships
Los Nombres de Cantidad	**72**	Nouns of Quantity
Los Adjetivos	**74**	Adjectives
Las Preposiciones	**76**	Prepositions
El Indice	**78**	Index

En el Espacio	**A.**	**In Space**	
el cometa	1	comet	
la constelación	2	constellation	
la galaxia	3	galaxy	
el planeta	4	planet	
la estrella	5	star	
la Luna	6	Moon	
la Tierra	7	Earth	
el Sol	8	Sun	
la órbita	9	orbit	

Las Fases de la Luna	**B.**	**Phases of the Moon**	
el eclipse	10	eclipse	

la luna nueva / creciente	11	new / crescent moon	
la media luna / el semilunio	12	half moon	
la luna llena	13	full moon	
el cuarto menguante	14	old moon	

Los Viajes Espaciales	**C.**	**Space Travel**	
la tobera propulsora	15	nosecone	
el cohete	16	rocket	
la plataforma de lanzamiento	17	launch(ing) pad	
el satélite	18	satellite	
la cápsula espacial	19	(space) capsule	
el astronauta	20	astronaut	
el traje espacial	21	spacesuit	

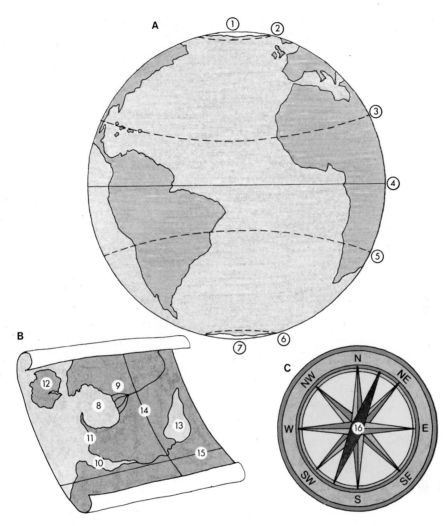

El Globo Terráqueo	**A.**	**Globe**		el lago	13	lake
el Polo Norte	1	North Pole		la longitud	14	line of longitude
el Círculo Artico	2	Arctic Circle		la latitud	15	line of latitude
el Trópico de Cáncer	3	Tropic of Cancer				
el Ecuador	4	Equator				
el Trópico de Capricornio	5	Tropic of Capricorn		Una Brújula	**C.**	**Compass**
el Círculo Antártico	6	Antarctic Circle		la aguja	16	needle
el Polo Sur	7	South Pole		N el norte		N north
				NE el nordeste/noreste		NE northeast
				E el este		E east
Un Mapa	**B.**	**Map**		SE el sudeste/sureste		SE southeast
la bahía/la ensenada	8	bay		S el sur/sud		S south
el delta	9	delta		SW el sudoeste/suroeste		SW southwest
el estuario	10	estuary		W el oeste		W west
la costa	11	coastline		NW el noroeste		NW northwest
la isla	12	island				

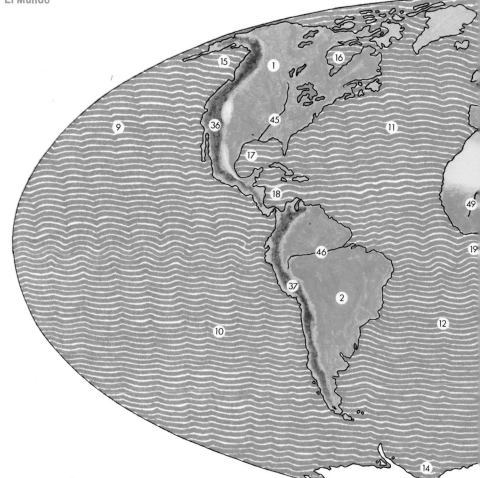

Los Continentes	**Continents**		Los Mares, Los Golfos,	**Seas, Gulfs, Bays**	
Norteamérica	1	North America	**Las Bahías**		
Sudamérica/Suramérica	2	South America	el Golfo de Alaska	15	Gulf of Alaska
Europa	3	Europe	la Bahía de Hudson	16	Hudson Bay
Africa	4	Africa	el Golfo de México	17	Gulf of Mexico
Asia	5	Asia	el Mar Caribe	18	Caribbean Sea
Australia	6	Australia	el Golfo de Guinea	19	Gulf of Guinea
Antártica	7	Antarctica	el Mar del Norte	20	North Sea
			el Mar Báltico	21	Baltic Sea
			el Mar Mediterráneo	22	Mediterranean Sea
Los Océanos	**Oceans**		el Mar Negro	23	Black Sea
el Artico	8	Arctic	el Mar Caspio	24	Caspian Sea
el Pacífico del Norte	9	North Pacific	el Mar Rojo	25	Red Sea
el Pacífico del Sur	10	South Pacific	el Golfo de Persa	26	Persian Gulf
el Atlántico del Norte	11	North Atlantic	el Mar Arabe	27	Arabian Sea
el Atlántico del Sur	12	South Atlantic	el Golfo de Bengala	28	Bay of Bengal
el Indico	13	Indian	el Mar de Coral	29	Coral Sea
el Antártico	14	Southern	el Mar de Tasmania	30	Tasman Sea

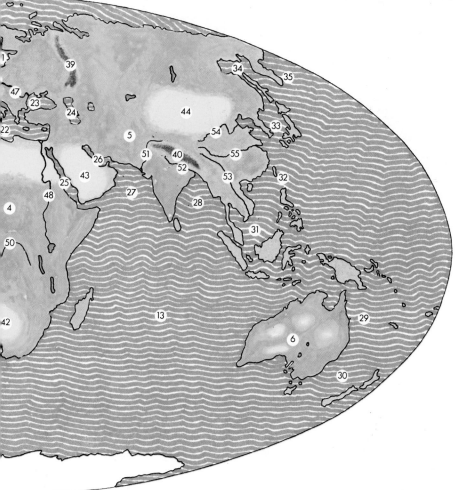

el Mar de China Meridional	31	South China Sea	
el Mar de China Oriental	32	East China Sea	
el Mar del Japón	33	Sea of Japan	
el Mar de Ujostk	34	Sea of Okhotsk	
el Mar de Bering	35	Bering Sea	

Las Cadenas Montañosas	**Mountain Ranges**	
las Montañas Roqueñas	36	Rockies
los Andes	37	Andes
los Alpes	38	Alps
los Montes Urales	39	Urals
el Himalaya	40	Himalayas

Los Desiertos	**Deserts**	
el Sahara	41	Sahara
el Kalahari	42	Kalahari

el desierto Arabe	43	Arabian
el Gobi	44	Gobi

Los Ríos	**Rivers**	
el Misisipi	45	Mississippi
el Amazonas	46	Amazon
el Danubio	47	Danube
el Nilo	48	Nile
el Níger	49	Niger
el Congo	50	Congo
el Indo	51	Indus
el Ganges	52	Ganges
el Mekong	53	Mekong
el Hoang Ho/el Amarillo	54	Yellow
el Yang Tse/el Azul	55	Yangtze

A

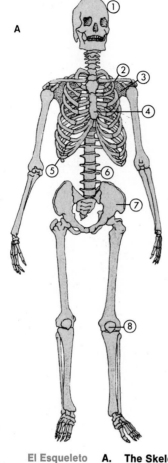

B

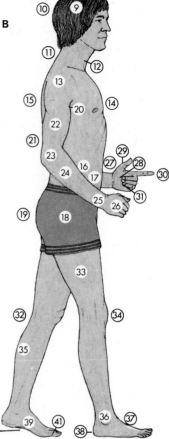

El Esqueleto	A.	The Skeleton
el cráneo/la calavera	1	skull
la clavícula	2	collar bone
el omóplato	3	shoulder blade
el esternón	4	breastbone
la costilla	5	rib
la espina dorsal	6	backbone/spine
la cadera/la pelvis	7	hip bone/pelvis
la rótula	8	kneecap

El Cuerpo	B.	The Body
el cabello/el pelo	9	hair
la cabeza	10	head
el cuello	11	neck
la garganta	12	throat
el hombro	13	shoulder
el pecho	14	chest
la espalda	15	back
la cintura	16	waist
el estómago	17	stomach

la cadera	18	hip
las nalgas	19	buttocks
la axila/el sobaco	20	armpit
el brazo	21	arm
la parte superior del brazo	22	upper arm
el codo	23	elbow
el antebrazo	24	forearm
la muñeca	25	wrist
el puño	26	fist
la mano	27	hand
la palma	28	palm
el pulgar	29	thumb
el dedo	30	finger
la uña	31	nail/fingernail
la pierna	32	leg
el muslo	33	thigh
la rodilla	34	knee
la pantorrilla	35	calf
el tobillo	36	ankle
el pie	37	foot

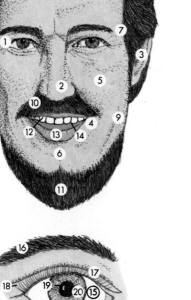

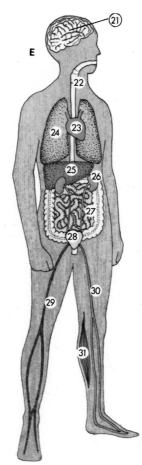

el talón	38	heel
el empeine	39	instep
la planta del pie	40	sole
el dedo del pie	41	toe

La Cara	**C.**	**The Face**
el ojo	1	eye
la nariz	2	nose
la oreja	3	ear
la boca	4	mouth
la mejilla/el cachete	5	cheek
el mentón/la barbilla	6	chin
la sien	7	temple
la frente	8	forehead
la quijada/la mandíbula	9	jaw
el bigote	10	mustache
la barba	11	beard
el diente	12	tooth
el labio	13	lip
la lengua	14	tongue

El Ojo	**D.**	**The Eye**
el globo ocular	15	eyeball
la ceja	16	eyebrow
el párpado	17	eyelid
las pestañas	18	eyelashes
la pupila	19	pupil
el iris	20	iris

Los Organos Internos	**E.**	**The Insides**
el cerebro	21	brain
la tráquea	22	windpipe
el corazón	23	heart
el pulmón	24	lung
el hígado	25	liver
el riñón	26	kidney
los intestinos	27	intestines
la vejiga	28	bladder
la vena	29	vein
la arteria	30	artery
el músculo	31	muscle

la bata	1	bathrobe	el zapato	11	shoe
el pijama	2	pajamas	la bota de lluvia	12	rubber boot
la zapatilla/la pantufla	3	slipper	los tenis	13	sneaker/tennis sho
la camiseta	4	undershirt/T-shirt	los mahones/	14	jeans
los calzoncillos	5	(under)shorts	los mecánicos		
la media/el calcetín	6	sock	el suéter	15	sweater
la chaqueta/el saco	7	jacket/sport coat	la correa/el cinturón	16	belt
los pantalones	8	slacks	la hebilla	17	buckle
el suéter abierto	9	(cardigan) sweater	la bota	18	boot
el zapato/el mocasín	10	loafer	la chaqueta	19	jacket

la camisa	1	shirt	los pantalones	17	trousers/pants
el cuello	2	collar	la vuelta/el doblez	18	cuff
el puño	3	cuff	la bufanda	19	scarf
la corbata	4	tie	el guante	20	glove
el chaleco	5	vest	el reloj	21	watch
el traje	6	suit	la correa	22	watchband
la manga	7	sleeve	los anteojos/los lentes/	23	glasses
el zapato	8	shoe	los espejuelos		
el cordón/la cinta de zapato	9	shoelace	el paraguas	24	umbrella
la suela	10	sole	las juntas/los yugos/	25	cuff links
el taco/el tacón	11	heel	las mancuernas		
la capa de agua/			el botón	26	button
el impermeable	12	trenchcoat/raincoat	la chaqueta/el saco	27	jacket/sport coat
el sombrero	13	hat	el maletín	28	briefcase
el abrigo/el sobretodo	14	overcoat/coat	los pantalones	29	slacks
la solapa	15	lapel	el sombrero de lluvia	30	rain hat
el bolsillo	16	pocket			

el sostén/el brasier	1	bra
la enagua/el fondo	2	slip
los calzones/las bragas/ las pantaletas	3	panties
las pantimedias/las medias panties	4	panty hose
el camisón	5	nightgown
la pantufla/la chancleta/ la zapatilla	6	slipper
el anillo/la sortija	7	ring
la pulsera/el brazalete	8	bracelet
el arete/la pantalla	9	earring
el collar	10	necklace
la lima de uñas	11	nail file
el polvo compacto	12	compact
el rímel para las pestañas	13	mascara
el esmalte de uñas	14	nail polish
el perfume/la esencia	15	perfume
la sombra para ojos	16	eye shadow
la crema de cara	17	face cream
el lápiz de labios	18	lipstick
la peinilla/el peine	19	comb
el cepillo	20	brush
la bata	21	bathrobe
el rolo/el enrizador	22	roller
el pinche	23	clip

el suéter	1	turtleneck sweater	el vestido/el traje	10	dress
el traje pantalón	2	pantsuit	el abrigo	11	coat
la bota	3	boot	la media	12	(knee) sock
la cartera/el bolso	4	(shoulder) bag/purse	la orquilla	13	barrette
el traje	5	suit	los mahones/	14	jeans
la blusa	6	blouse	los mecánicos		
la chaqueta	7	(suit) jacket	la camisa	15	shirt
la falda	8	skirt	el suéter	16	sweater
el pañuelo	9	handkerchief	la sandalia	17	sandal

el buzón	1	mailbox	la cuneta	9	gutter
el paso de peatones	2	crosswalk	la alcantarilla/el desagüe	10	drain/sewer
la estación de tren	3	subway station	el parque	11	park
el taxi	4	taxi/taxicab	el puente	12	bridge
la bicicleta	5	bicycle	la camioneta	13	van
el semáforo	6	traffic light	el camión	14	truck
el rótulo	7	street sign	el cruce	15	intersection
la acera/la banqueta	8	curb	la motocicleta/la motoneta	16	motorcycle

el coche/el carrito del bebé	17	baby carriage
el edificio de apartamientos	18	apartment house
el edificio de oficinas	19	office building
la tienda	20	store
la vitrina/el escaparate	21	display window
el farol	22	street light
el metro/el parquímetro	23	parking meter
el autobús/el camión/ la guagua	24	bus
la parada de autobús	25	bus stop
la acera/la banqueta	26	sidewalk
el safacón/el latón/ el bote de basura	27	trash can
la cabina telefónica	28	telephone booth
el estacionamiento	29	parking lot
el coche/el carro/ la máquina	30	car
la calle/la carretera	31	street/road

Identificación	**A.**	**Detection**
el policía	1	policeman
el revólver/la pistola	2	gun
el uniforme	3	uniform
el cuartel de policía/	4	police station
la comisaría		
la patrulla/el patrullero	5	police car
el perro policía	6	police dog
el garrote	7	nightstick
las esposas	8	handcuffs
la linterna	9	flashlight
la lupa	10	magnifying glass
las huellas digitales	11	fingerprints
las huellas	12	footprints

La Cárcel	**B.**	**Jail**
el carcelero/el guardia penal	13	guard
el preso	14	prisoner
la celda	15	cell
las rejas	16	bars

La Corte de Justicia	**C.**	**Court of Law**
el jurado	17	jury
la tribuna de los testigos	18	witness stand
el testigo	19	witness
el acusado	20	defendant/accused
el abogado defensor	21	defense attorney
el juez	22	judge
el fiscal	23	prosecuting attorney
la toga	24	gown/robe
el taquígrafo	25	stenographer

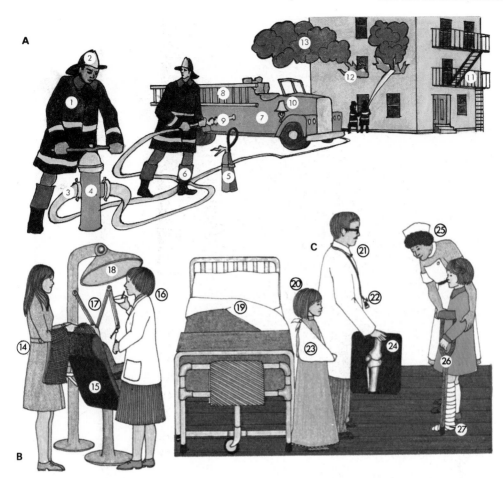

El Cuartel de Bomberos/	**A.**	**Fire Department**
El Parque de Bombas		
el bombero	1	fireman
el casco	2	fireman's hat
la manguera	3	(fire) hose
el hidrante	4	(fire) hydrant
el extinguidor de incendios	5	fire extinguisher
la bota	6	(fireman's) boot
el camión de bomberos	7	fire engine/truck
la escalera extensible	8	ladder
la boquilla de manguera	9	nozzle
la campana	10	bell
la escalera de escape	11	fire escape
el incendio/el fuego	12	fire
el humo	13	smoke
Con el Dentista	**B.**	**At the Dentist**
la ayudante	14	dental assistant

el sillón	15	dentist's chair
el dentista	16	dentist
el taladro	17	drill
la lámpara	18	lamp/light
Una Sala de Hospital	**C.**	**A Hospital Ward**
la cama	19	(hospital) bed
el paciente	20	patient
el médico/el doctor	21	doctor
el estetoscopio	22	stethoscope
el cabestrillo	23	sling
la radiografía	24	X-ray
la enfermera	25	nurse
las muletas	26	crutches
la venda/el vendaje	27	bandage

la maestra	1	teacher	el compás	11	compass
la pizarra/el pizarrón	2	blackboard	el transportador	12	protractor
el borrador	3	eraser	la goma de pegar/la pega	13	glue
la tiza	4	chalk	el libro	14	book
la alumna/la estudiante	5	student	el cuaderno	15	notebook
el bulto/la mochila	6	book bag	la regla de cálculo	16	slide rule
el escritorio/el pupitre	7	desk	la hoja de papel	17	loose-leaf paper
el lápiz	8	pencil	la carpeta (de papeles)	18	loose-leaf notebook
la pluma	9	pen	el mapa	19	map
la regla	10	ruler	el calendario	20	calendar

la balanza	1	scales	el mechero de Bunsen	12	Bunsen burner
el platillo	2	pan	el trípode	13	tripod
las pesas	3	weights	el tubo de goma	14	rubber tubing
el contador	4	meter	el vaso de precipitación	15	beaker
la carátula/el cuadrante	5	dial	el frasco/el matraz	16	flask
la aguja/la mano	6	needle/pointer	los cristales	17	crystals
el banco	7	bench	la pipeta	18	pipette
el banquito	8	stool	el imán	19	magnet
el microscópio	9	microscope	la mano del mortero	20	pestle
los lentes	10	lens	el mortero	21	mortar
la platina/la laminilla	11	slide	el tubo de ensayo	22	test tube

el carrito	1	shopping cart	el estante/el tablillero	15	shelf
la cajera	2	cashier	la comida de lata	16	canned food
la caja registradora	3	cash register	las frutas	17	fruit
el mostrador de la caja	4	checkout counter	los vegetales/las verduras	18	vegetables
el cliente	5	customer	el pan	19	bread
la bolsa/la jaba	6	sack/bag	las galletitas	20	cookies
el cesto/la canasta	7	(shopping) basket	el bizcocho/el pastel	21	cake
el dependiente/el vendedor	8	clerk	el pescado	22	fish
el queso	9	cheese	el recibo	23	receipt
la leche	10	milk	los billetes	24	bills
los huevos	11	eggs	las monedas	25	coins
las salchichas	12	hot dogs	las galletas	26	crackers
la carne	13	meat	las papas	27	potatoes
el congelador	14	freezer	el polvo de jabón/ el detergente	28	soap powder

el escritorio	1	desk	el conmutador	15	switchboard
el teléfono	2	telephone	la operadora	16	operator
la calculadora	3	calculator	el calendario	17	calendar
el papel secante	4	blotter	el cartapacio	18	file
el libro de citas	5	appointment book	el archivo	19	file/filing cabinet
la perforadora	6	hole puncher	el papel carbón	20	carbon paper
a engrapadora/la presilladora	7	stapler	la máquina de escribir/	21	typewriter
la máquina de sumar	8	adding machine	la maquinilla		
la presilla	9	paper clip	la secretaria	22	secretary
el tablón de edictos/avisos	10	bulletin board	el cuaderno/la libreta	23	steno pad
el sobre	11	envelope	el estante para libros	24	bookcase
a caja para la correspondencia	12	in-box	la recepcionista	25	receptionist
el safacón/el bote de basura	13	wastepaper basket	el fichero	26	card file
la máquina de sacar cópias	14	photocopier	el lapicero	27	pencil holder

el empleado de correos	1	postal clerk	la dirección de retorno	12	return address
la balanza/el pesacartas	2	scale	la zona postal	13	zip code
el mostrador	3	counter	la tarjeta postal	14	postcard
el buzón	4	mailbox	el sobre	15	envelope
el cartero	5	mailman	la solapa del sobre	16	flap
el saco de correspondencia	6	mailbag	el telegrama/el cable	17	telegram/cable
el aerograma	7	aerogram	el giro/el cheque postal	18	money order
el sello impreso	8	postmark	el paquete	19	package
el sello/el timbre/la estampilla	9	stamp	el cordón/el cordel	20	string
el sobre aéreo	10	(airmail) envelope	la etiqueta	21	label
la dirección	11	address			

la grúa	1	crane	el obrero	14	workman
el albañil	2	bricklayer	la arena	15	sand
las vigas	3	rafters	el cemento	16	cement
la teja	4	shingle	el traspalador/el palaústre	17	trowel
la escalera	5	ladder	el cuezo	18	hod
el escalón/el peldaño	6	rung	el nivel	19	level
el andamio	7	scaffolding	la excavadora	20	excavator
los ladrillos	8	bricks	la mezcladora de cemento/	21	cement mixer
la cañería	9	drainpipe	la hormigonera		
los cimientos	10	foundations	el camión de volteo	22	dump truck
el tablón	11	board	la perforadora de aire	23	pneumatic drill
el pico	12	pick(ax)	comprimido		
la pala	13	shovel	la carretilla	24	wheelbarrow

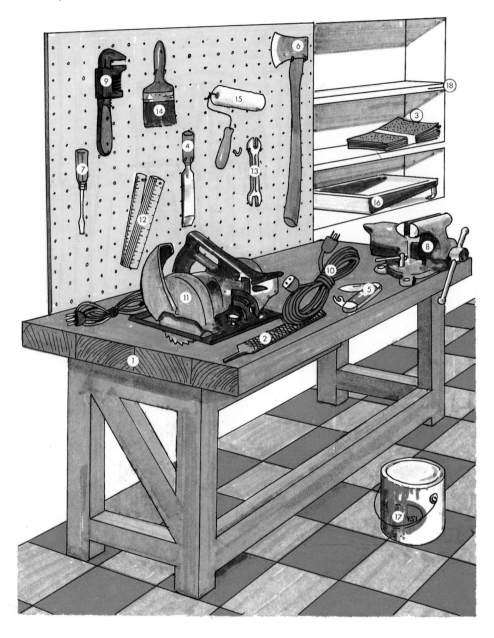

el banco de trabajo	1	workbench	la extensión eléctrica	10	extension cord
la lima	2	file	el serrucho eléctrico	11	power saw
el papel de lija	3	sandpaper	el metro	12	folding rule
el formón/el cincel	4	chisel	la llave	13	wrench
la cuchilla/la navaja	5	pocket knife	la brocha	14	paintbrush
el hacha	6	axe	el rodillo de pintura	15	(paint) roller
el destornillador	7	screwdriver	el azafate de pintura	16	(paint) pan
la prensa	8	vise	el pote/la lata de pintura	17	paint can
la llave inglesa	9	monkey wrench	la tablilla/el estante	18	shelf

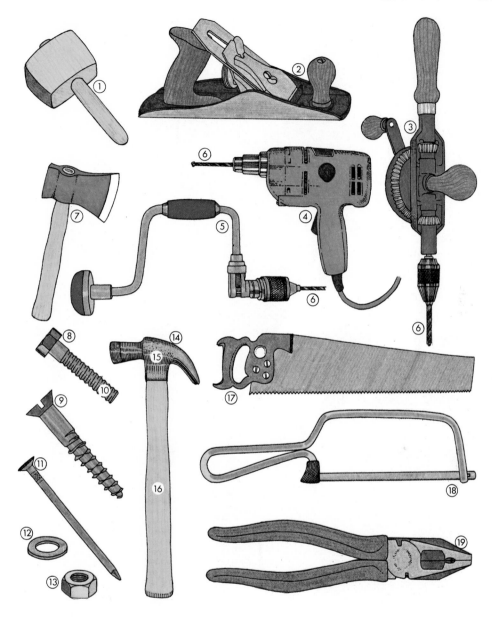

el mazo cuadrado	1	mallet
el cepillo del carpintero	2	plane
el taladro de mano	3	hand drill
el taladro eléctrico	4	electric drill
el berbiquí	5	brace
la barrena/ el taladro	6	bit
el hacha	7	hatchet
el perno	8	bolt
el tornillo de rosca	9	screw
la rosca	10	thread

el clavo	11	nail
la arandela	12	washer
la tuerca	13	nut
el martillo	14	hammer
la cabeza del martillo	15	head
el mango del martillo	16	handle
el serrucho	17	saw
la sierra/ la segueta	18	hacksaw
la tenaza/ el alicate	19	pliers

el techo	1	roof		la persiana	12	shutter
la chimenea	2	chimney		la jardinera	13	window box
la pared	3	(outside) wall		la cortina	14	curtain
el balcón	4	balcony		la persiana	15	blind
el patio	5	patio		el canal de desagüe	16	gutter
el garaje	6	garage		el desagüe	17	drainpipe
la puerta de entrada/la entrada	7	(front) door		la alfombrilla/el tapetito	18	doormat
la ventana	8	window		la antena	19	antenna/aerial
el marco de la ventana	9	window frame		el cobertizo para	20	(tool) shed
el vidrio de la ventana	10	windowpane		herramientas		
el alféizar/el alero	11	(window)sill		el pasto/la hierba	21	grass

El Tiempo	**The Weather**		las hojas	15	leaves
el relámpago	1	lightning	el portón	16	gate
el nubarrón/	2	(storm)cloud	la cerca	17	hedge
la nube de tormenta			el camino/el sendero/	18	path
la lluvia	3	rain	la vereda		
las gotas de lluvia	4	raindrops	el césped/la grama	19	lawn
la nieve	5	snow	la flor	20	flower
la bola de nieve	6	snowball	el jardín de flores/el macizo	21	flower bed
el hombre de nieve	7	snowman	el arbusto	22	bush
el carámbano	8	icicle	la regadera	23	watering can
el sol	9	sun	el tiesto/la maceta	24	flower pot
el cielo	10	sky	la horquilla/el tenedor	25	pitchfork
			el cobertizo	26	shed
En el Patio	**In the Yard**		la carretilla	27	wheelbarrow
el árbol	11	tree	la cuerda para colgar ropa	28	clothesline
el tronco	12	trunk	la ropa lavada	29	laundry
la rama	13	branch	la pinza	30	clothespin
las ramitas	14	twigs			

la puerta	1	door	la escalera	12	staircase
el llamador/la aldaba	2	mail slot	la barandilla/la baranda	13	banister
la cerradura de seguridad	3	lock and chain	la planta alta	14	upstairs
el cerrojo	4	bolt	la planta baja	15	downstairs
la bisagra	5	hinge	la luz	16	light
el tapetito/la alfombrilla	6	(door)mat	el apagador/el chucho	17	(light) switch
el piso	7	floor	el teléfono	18	telephone/phone
la alfombra	8	rug	el receptor (auricular)	19	receiver
el perchero	9	(coat)rack	el disco	20	dial
el gancho	10	hook	el cordón del teléfono	21	cord
el escalón	11	stair	la guía telefónica	22	telephone book

el techo/el cielo	1	ceiling	el librero	16	bookcase
la pared	2	wall	la tabla	17	shelf
la alfombra	3	carpet	el amplificador	18	amplifier
la chimenea	4	fireplace	el tocadiscos	19	turntable
la repisa de la chimenea	5	mantel	la bocina	20	speaker
el fuego	6	fire	el disco	21	record
la cortina	7	curtain	la carpeta	22	(record) jacket
la cortina/el portier	8	drape	la mesita	23	coffee table
el sofá	9	couch/sofa	la radio	24	radio
el cojín/el almohadón	10	cushion	la mesita	25	end table
el sillón	11	armchair	la lámpara	26	lamp
el periódico	12	newspaper	la pantalla	27	lampshade
la silla	13	chair	la televisión/el televisor	28	television/TV
el anaquel para las revistas	14	magazine rack	el cenicero	29	ashtray
la revista	15	magazine			

la estufa/la cocina	1	stove	el abrelatas	21	can opener
el horno	2	oven	la lata	22	can
la parilla	3	broiler	el abridor de botellas	23	bottle opener
la hornilla/el quemador	4	burner	la máquina de lavar platos	24	dishwasher
la nevera/el refrigerador	5	refrigerator	el secador de platos	25	dish towel
el gabinete	6	cabinet	la mesa	26	table
el fregadero/la pileta	7	sink	la silla	27	chair
el mostrador/el tablero	8	counter	la servilleta	28	napkin
el safacón/el bote de basura	9	garbage can	el portaservilletas	29	napkin holder
la canasta de frutas	10	fruit basket	el mantel individual	30	place mat
las frutas	11	fruit	el cuchillo	31	knife
la olla/la cacerola/la cazuela	12	pot	la cuchara	32	spoon
el sartén	13	pan	el tenedor	33	fork
el sartén	14	skillet/frying pan	el plato	34	plate
la panera	15	bread box	el plato hondo	35	bowl
la tablilla/el estante	16	shelf	el vaso	36	glass
la tetera	17	(tea) kettle	la taza	37	cup
la tostadora	18	toaster	el azucarero	38	sugar bowl
el abrelatas eléctrico	19	electric can opener	el salero	39	saltshaker
el cafetero	20	coffee pot	la pimentera	40	pepper shaker

la aspiradora	1	vacuum cleaner	el cordón	12	cord
la escoba	2	broom	la bombilla/el foco/	13	(light)bulb
la tabla (de planchar)	3	ironing board	el bombillo		
la lavadora eléctrica	4	washing machine	el secador de pelo	14	hair dryer
el mapo	5	mop	el enchufe/la clavija/	15	plug
la escobilla de mano	6	dust brush	el enchufle		
el trapo	7	dustcloth	el tomacorriente/el enchufe/	16	outlet/socket
el recogedor	8	dustpan	el enchufle		
el polvo limpiador	9	scouring powder	el apagador/el chucho	17	switch
el cepillo	10	scrub brush	el jabón detergente (en polvo)	18	soap powder
la plancha	11	iron	el cubo/el balde/la cubeta	19	pail/bucket

El Dormitorio/La Recámara	**The Bedroom**		el cepillo (para pelo)	21	hair brush

El Dormitorio/La Recámara **The Bedroom**

la cama	1	bed
la cabecera	2	headboard
la almohada	3	pillow
la funda	4	pillowcase
la sábana	5	sheet
la frisa/la manta/la cobija/ la frazada	6	blanket
la colcha/la sobrecama/ la cubrecama	7	bedspread
el colchón	8	mattress
la mesa de noche	9	night table
el tocador	10	dressing table
el volante del tocador	11	dressing table skirt
el banquito/el taburete	12	stool
el espejo	13	mirror
el armario/el closet/el ropero	14	closet
el escritorio	15	desk
el gabetero/la cómoda	16	chest of drawers
la alfombrilla/el tapete	17	rug
el cajón para los juguetes	18	toy box
el juguete	19	toy
el juego	20	game

el cepillo (para pelo)	21	hair brush
la peinilla/el peine	22	comb
los pañuelos desechables	23	box of tissues
el joyero/el alhajero/ el estuche	24	jewelry box
el reloj despertador	25	alarm clock

El Bebé **The Baby**

la cuna	26	crib
el camisón de dormir	27	sleeper
el bobo/el chupón/ el chupete	28	pacifier
el muñeco de peluche	29	stuffed animal
el sonajero/la maraquita/ la sonaja	30	rattle
la muñeca	31	doll
el catre de baño	32	changing table
la botella/el biberón	33	bottle
la mamadera/el chupón	34	nipple
el babero	35	bib
el pañal	36	diaper
el polvo del bebe	37	baby powder

la bañera/la tina	1	bathtub/tub
la llave de agua caliente	2	hot water faucet
la llave de agua fría	3	cold water faucet
la ducha/la regadera	4	shower head
el desagüe	5	drain
el tapón de desagüe	6	drain plug
el selector de ducha	7	diverter
el inodoro/el excusado	8	toilet
la cadena/la manga/el mango	9	handle
el papel higiénico (de baño)	10	toilet paper
el botiquín	11	medicine chest
el lavamano/el lavabo/la pileta	12	sink
la máquina de afeitar	13	razor
la navaja	14	(razor) blade
el envase para la crema de afeitar	15	shaving mug
el cepillo de afeitar	16	shaving brush

el cepillo de dientes	17	toothbrush
el vaso	18	glass
la toallita	19	washcloth
el cepillo de uñas	20	nail brush
la pasta de dientes	21	toothpaste
la toalla	22	towel
el toallero	23	towel rack
la romana/la balanza/la escala	24	(bathroom) scale
la alfombrilla de baño	25	bath mat
la esponja	26	sponge
el jabón	27	soap
el cesto para la ropa sucia	28	hamper
la loseta	29	tile
el pasador de cortinas	30	curtain rod
la cortina de la bañera	31	shower curtain

la meseta/la altiplanicie	1	plateau	el prado/la pradera	11	meadow
la montaña	2	mountain	el río	12	river
la cúspide/la cima	3	(mountain) peak	el campo/la campiña	13	field
las cataratas	4	waterfall	el seto/el vallado de zarzas	14	hedge
el lago	5	lake	el árbol	15	tree
el valle	6	valley	la aldea/el pueblito	16	village
el arroyo/el riachuelo	7	stream	el sendero/el camino/	17	(foot)path
el bosque	8	wood	la vereda		
el bosque	9	forest	la carretera	18	road
la colina/la loma	10	hill	el estanque/la charca	19	pond

tienda de campaña/la carpa	1	tent	la silla de playa	19	deck chair

tienda de campaña/la carpa — 1 tent
piso de la tienda/de la carpa — 2 groundcloth
la bolsa de dormir — 3 sleeping bag
la mochila — 4 backpack
la hornilla para acampar — 5 camp(ing) stove
el acantilado — 6 cliff
el hotel — 7 hotel
la quinta/la casita de campo — 8 cottage
el paseo/el malecón — 9 boardwalk
la muralla — 10 seawall
la playa — 11 beach
el quitasol/la sombrilla de playa — 12 beach umbrella
la persona tomando sol — 13 sunbather
la toalla (de playa) — 14 (beach) towel
los anteojos submarinos — 15 mask/goggles
el tubo de respiración/el snorkel — 16 snorkel
el helado — 17 ice cream
la mampara/el rompeviento — 18 windbreaker

la silla de playa — 19 deck chair
el traje de baño/la trusa — 20 bathing trunks
la aleta — 21 flipper
la arena — 22 sand
el castillo de arena — 23 sandcastle
el balde/el cubo/la cubeta — 24 bucket
la pala — 25 shovel
la pelota de playa — 26 beach ball
la concha — 27 seashell
los guijarros/las piedras lisas — 28 pebbles
las rocas — 29 rocks
el cometa/el papalote/la chiringa — 30 kite
el agua — 31 water
el oleaje — 32 surf
la ola — 33 wave
la lancha de motor — 34 motorboat
la bañista/el nadador — 35 swimmer
la ropa de baño — 36 bathing suit
el alga — 37 seaweed

el henil	1	hayloft	el tractor	18	tractor
el heno	2	hay	el arado	19	plow
el establo para reses	3	cow shed	el surco	20	furrow
el establo	4	barn	la vaca	21	cow
el corral	5	pen	el ternero/el becerro	22	calf
el corralón	6	barnyard	el toro	23	bull
la casa (del rancho)	7	farm house	las cabras	24	goats
el campo	8	field	el caballo	25	horse
el abrevadero/el estanque del corral	9	pond	la crin	26	mane
			la herradura	27	hoof
la cerca	10	fence	la silla de montar	28	saddle
el árbol frutal	11	fruit tree	la oveja	29	sheep
el huerto	12	orchard	el cordero	30	lamb
el espantapájaros	13	scarecrow	el patito	31	duckling
el trigo	14	wheat	el pato	32	duck
el granjero	15	farmer	la gallina/el pollo	33	hen/chicken
el mezclador	16	combine	el gallo	34	rooster
el caz/la acequía	17	irrigation canal	el pollito/el polluelo	35	chick

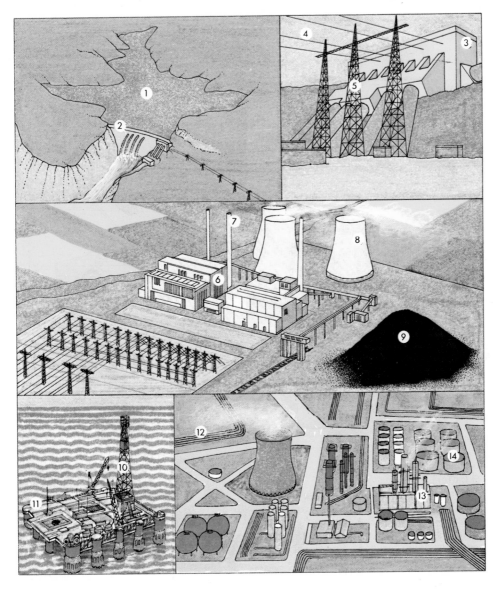

el depósito/la cisterna	1	reservoir
el dique/la represa	2	dam
la central eléctrica	3	powerhouse
el cable de energía eléctrica	4	cable
la torre de conducción eléctrica	5	pylon
la estación de energía eléctrica	6	power station
la chimenea	7	smokestack
la torre de enfriamiento	8	cooling tower
el carbón	9	coal
la instalación petrolera	10	derrick
el ajustador petrolero	11	oil-rig
el oleoducto/la tubería	12	pipeline
la refinería	13	refinery
el depósito	14	storage tank

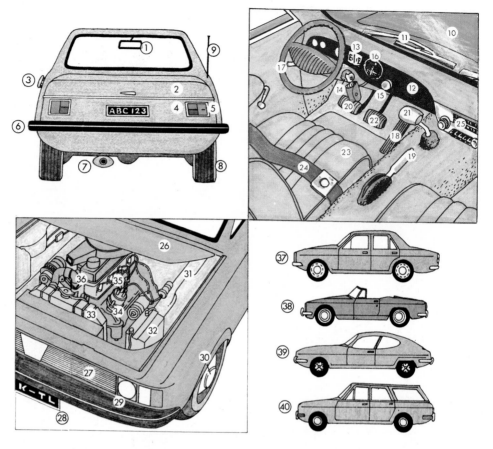

El Automóvil/El Coche/ El Carro/La Máquina	**The Car**		el embrague/el cloche	20	clutch
el espejo retrovisor	1	rearview mirror	la palanca de velocidades	21	gearshift
la cajuela/el baúl/la maleta	2	trunk	el freno	22	brake
el tapón de la gasolina	3	gas cap	el asiento	23	seat
la luz trasera/el farol de cola	4	taillight	el cinturón de seguridad	24	seat/safety belt
la luz indicadora/la direccional	5	turn signal	el radio (de automóvil)	25	car radio
la defensa	6	bumper	la capota/la tapa	26	hood
el tubo de escape/el mofile	7	exhaust	la plancha del radiador	27	grill
la llanta/el neumático/la goma	8	tire	la placa (de matrícula)/ la chapa	28	license plate
la antena	9	antenna/aerial	el farol delantero	29	headlight
el parabrisas	10	windshield	el tapón/el tapabocina	30	hubcap
el limpiaparabrisas	11	windshield wiper	el motor	31	engine
el tablero (de mandos)/ la pizarra	12	dashboard	la batería/el acumulador	32	battery
			el radiador	33	radiator
el medidor de gasolina	13	fuel/gas gauge	el distribuidor	34	distributor
el encendido/la ignición	14	ignition	la bujía	35	spark plug
el obturador de aire	15	choke	la cabeza del cilindro	36	cylinder head
el velocímetro	16	speedometer	el sedán	37	sedan
el volante/el guía/el timón	17	steering wheel	el descapotable/el convertible	38	convertible
el acelerador	18	accelerator	el cupé	39	sports coupe
el freno (de mano)	19	hand/emergency brake	la camioneta	40	station wagon

la autopista	1	thruway/freeway/ expressway
el paso superior/el viaducto	2	overpass
el paso subterráneo	3	underpass
la rotonda (de tráfico)/el círculo	4	circle
el carril exterior	5	left/outside lane
el carril interior	6	right/inside lane
la estación de servicio/ la gasolinera	7	gas station
la bomba de gasolina/ el surtidor	8	gas pump
la bomba de aire	9	air pump
el encargado de la gasolinera	10	attendant
el camión (de remolque)	11	trailer truck
el camión de transporte	12	transporter
la casa remolcable	13	trailer
el camión de carga	14	truck
la ambulancia	15	ambulance
el automóvil/el coche/ el carro/la máquina	16	car
el camión de pasajeros/ la guagua	17	bus
el coche deportivo	18	sports car
el camión petrolero	19	oil truck
la motocicleta	20	motorcycle
el camión tractor	21	trailer
la camioneta/la furgoneta	22	van

la bicicleta	1	bicycle/bike
la campanilla/el timbre	2	bell
el espejo	3	mirror
el cable	4	cable
el farol delantero	5	headlight
el manubrio/el guía	6	handlebars
el asiento	7	seat
el portaequipajes	8	saddlebag
la rueda	9	wheel
el guardabarros/ el guardafangos	10	mudguard
la llanta/el neumático/la goma	11	tire
los rayos	12	spokes
la válvula	13	valve
el freno	14	brake
el travesaño	15	crossbar
la bomba	16	pump
el pedal	17	pedal
la cadena	18	chain
la rueda dentada/el piñón	19	sprocket
el reflector	20	reflector
la parada de taxi	21	taxi stand
el taxímetro/el taxi	22	taxi(cab)/cab
el metro	23	meter
el pasaje	24	fare
el taxista/el chofer	25	(taxi) driver
el pasajero	26	passenger
el casco	27	crash helmet
los anteojos de protección	28	goggles
la motoneta	29	motor scooter
el farol trasero/el farol de cola	30	rear light
el asiento	31	seat
el acelerador	32	accelerator
el freno	33	brake
el portaequipajes	34	saddlebag
el tubo de escape/el mofile	35	exhaust
el pedal de arranque	36	starter
el pedal	37	footrest
la palanca de velocidades	38	gearshift

el tren	1	train		el inspector	16	gateman
el maquinista	2	engineer		la barrera/el portón	17	gate
la máquina/la locomotora	3	engine		la sala de espera	18	waiting room
el vagón	4	coach		los pasajeros	19	passengers
el compartimiento de pasajeros	5	compartment		el andén/la plataforma	20	platform
el inspector de boletos	6	conductor		el número del andén	21	platform number
el boleto/el pasaje	7	ticket		el guardavía	22	signalman
el asiento	8	seat		la caseta de señales	23	signal box
la rejilla para equipaje	9	luggage rack		la vía (férrea)	24	(railroad) track
el guardafrenos	10	brakeman		los durmientes	25	(railroad) ties
la bandera	11	flag		las puntas	26	(railroad) switch
el pito/el silbato	12	whistle		las señales	27	signals
la estación	13	(train) station		el vagón de carga	28	freight car
la ventanilla de boletos	14	ticket office		el parachoques	29	buffer
el horario	15	schedule		el aparcadero/la vía muerta	30	siding

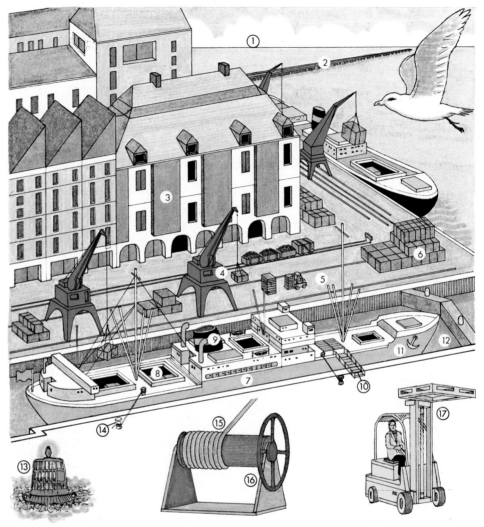

el horizonte	1	horizon	el pasadizo	10	gangway
el malecón	2	pier	el ancla	11	anchor
el almacén	3	warehouse	el muelle/el dique	12	dock
4 la grúa	4	crane	la boya	13	buoy
el muelle	5	wharf	el bolardo	14	bollard
la carga	6	cargo	el cable	15	cable
el barco	7	ship	el torno	16	windlass
la bodega	8	hold	el elevador de horquilla	17	forklift
la chimenea	9	smokestack			

el camarote/el crucero	1	sailboat	el motor fuera de borda	12	outboard motor
la vela	2	sail	la proa	13	bow
el mástil	3	mast	la popa	14	stern
el estabilizador	4	rudder	la lancha/el transbordador	15	ferry
la quilla	5	keel	la barcaza	16	barge
el bote de remar	6	rowboat	el buque pesquero	17	trawler
el remo	7	oar	el petrolero	18	tanker
la agarradera del remo	8	oarlock	la cubierta	19	deck
la canoa	9	canoe	el transatlántico	20	ocean liner
el remo de la canoa	10	paddle	la chimenea	21	smokestack
la lancha de motor	11	motorboat			

la aduana	1	customs	el ala	11	wing
el aduanero	2	customs officer	el motor de reacción	12	jet engine
el pasaporte	3	passport	la aleta	13	tail/tail fin
el equipaje	4	luggage/baggage	el planeador	14	glider
el comandante/el capitán/	5	captain/pilot	el helicóptero	15	helicopter
el piloto			el rotor/la turbina	16	rotor
el pasajero	6	passenger	la avioneta	17	light aircraft
la azafata/la aeromoza/	7	stewardess/	la hélice del aeroplano	18	propeller
la camarera		flight attendant	la pista	19	runway
el sobrecargo	8	steward/flight attendant	la torre de control	20	control tower
el avión de pasajeros	9	(air)plane/airliner	el hangar	21	hangar
el fuselaje	10	fuselage			

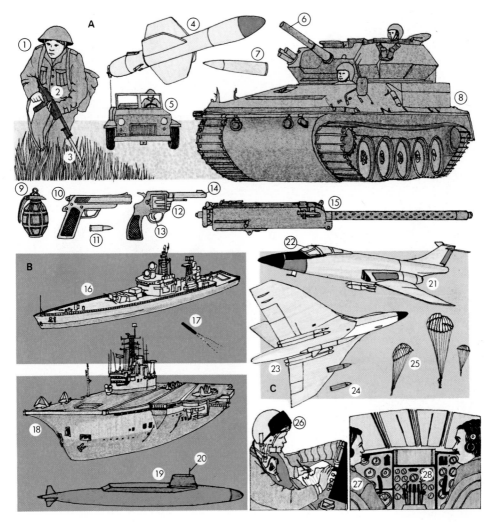

El Ejército	A.	Army
el soldado	1	soldier
la carabina/el rifle	2	rifle
la bayoneta	3	bayonet
el cohete teledirigido	4	guided missile
el jeep	5	jeep
el cañón	6	gun
el proyectil	7	shell
el tanque	8	tank
la granada de mano	9	(hand) grenade
la pistola	10	pistol
la bala/el cartucho	11	bullet/cartridge
el revólver	12	revolver
el gatillo/el disparador	13	trigger
el cañón	14	barrel
la ametralladora	15	machine gun

La Marina	B.	Navy
el buque de guerra	16	warship
el torpedo	17	torpedo
el portaaviones	18	aircraft carrier
el submarino	19	submarine
el periscopio	20	periscope

La Fuerza Aérea	C.	Air Force
el avión de caza/de combate	21	fighter plane
la cabina (del piloto)	22	cockpit
el bombardero	23	bomber
la bómba	24	bomb
el paracaídas	25	parachute
el navegante	26	navigator
el piloto (de avión)	27	pilot
el tablero de control	28	control panel

La Carrera de Caballos	**A.**	**(Horse) Racing**
el jockey	1	jockey
el caballo de carrera	2	(race)horse
la silla de montar	3	saddle
las riendas	4	reins
la brida	5	bridle
el freno	6	bit
el estribo	7	stirrup
los pantalones de equitación	8	jodhpurs
la gorra	9	cap

El Boxeo	**B.**	**Boxing**
el árbitro	10	referee
el boxeador	11	boxer
el guante	12	(boxing) glove
el cuadrilátero/el ring	13	ring
las cuerdas	14	ropes

El Basketball/El Baloncesto	**C.**	**Basketball**
el cesto	15	basket
el poste del tablero	16	backboard
la pelota	17	ball

El Hockey	**D.**	**Field Hockey**
el palo	18	stick

El Tenis de Mesa/ El Ping-Pong	**E.**	**Table-Tennis/ Ping-Pong**
la raqueta	19	racket
la red	20	net
la mesa	21	table

La Lucha	**F.**	**Wrestling**
los luchadores	22	wrestlers

El Judo	**G.**	**Judo**
el traje de judo	23	judo suit

El Fútbol Americano	**A.**	**Football**	el centro	15	center

El Fútbol Americano — **A. Football**

la pelota de fútbol	1	football
el yelmo/el casco	2	helmet
el árbitro	3	referee
la portería	4	goalpost

El Estadio — **B. Stadium**

la andanada/la gradería cubierta	5	(grand)stand
el campo/la cancha	6	field
las luces	7	lights

El Equipo de Jugadores — **C. Line-Up**

el guarda espalda/ el quarterback	8	quarterback
la defensa derecha	9	right halfback
la defensa trasera	10	fullback
la defensa izquierda	11	left halfback
la defensa extrema derecha	12	right end
el toque derecho	13	right tackle
el guardabosque derecho	14	right guard

el centro	15	center
el guardabosque izquierdo	16	left guard
el toque izquierdo	17	left tackle
la extrema izquierda	18	left end
la formación en T	19	T formation
la cadena	20	chain
el defensor de línea	21	linesman
la portería	22	goalpost
la pizarra/el tablero de puntuación	23	scoreboard
la ambulancia	24	ambulance

Deportes de Invierno — **D. Winter Sports**

el esquiador	25	skier
el esquí	26	ski
el palo de esquiar	27	(ski) pole
el piloto deslizador	28	tobogganist
el deslizador	29	toboggan
el patinador	30	(ice)skater
el patín	31	(ice)skate

El Beisbol	**Baseball**	
el bate	1	bat
el bateador	2	batter
el árbitro	3	umpire
el plato	4	home plate
el receptor	5	catcher
la máscara protectora	6	catcher's mask
el guante	7	mitt/glove
el lanzador	8	pitcher
la primera base	9	first base
el jugador de primera base	10	first baseman
el jugador de segunda base	11	second baseman
el torpedero	12	shortstop
el jugador de tercera base	13	third baseman
la línea foul	14	foul line
el jardinero izquierdo	15	left fielder
el jardinero del centro	16	center fielder
el jardinero derecho	17	right fielder

La Pesca	**Fishing**	
el pescador	18	fisherman
la caña de pescar	19	(fishing) rod
la cuerda	20	line
el anzuelo	21	hook
la carnada	22	bait

El Tenis	**Tennis**	
la cancha (de tenis)	23	(tennis) court
la red	24	net
el jugador con el saque	25	server
la línea de saque	26	service line
la raqueta de tenis	27	(tennis) racket
la pelota de tenis	28	(tennis) ball

La Orquesta	**Orchestra**		el pedal	17	**pedal**
el clarinete	1	**clarinet**	el taburete	18	**stool**
la válvula	2	**valve**	la trompeta	19	**trumpet**
el músico	3	**musician/player**	el trombón	20	**trombone**
el violín	4	**violin**	la vara corredora	21	**slide**
las cuerdas	5	**strings**	el saxofón	22	**saxophone**
el arco	6	**bow**	la embocadura/la boquilla	23	**mouthpiece**
la viola	7	**viola**			
el violoncelo	8	**cello**			
el contrabajo	9	**double bass**	**El Conjunto de Música Popular**		**Pop Group**
el director de orquesta	10	**conductor**	el cantante	24	**singer**
la batuta	11	**baton**	el micrófono	25	**microphone**
la partitura	12	**(sheet) music**	la guitarra eléctrica	26	**(electric) guitar**
el estrado	13	**rostrum**	el amplificador	27	**amplifier**
el cuerno inglés	14	**horn**	el autoparlante/el altavoz	28	**(loud)speaker**
el piano	15	**piano**	los platillos	29	**cymbals**
las teclas	16	**keys**	el tambor	30	**drum**

El Teatro	**A.**	**The Theater**		El Cine	**B.**	**The Movies**
el escenario	1	stage		el cuarto de proyección	14	projection room
el actor	2	actor		el proyector	15	projector
la actriz	3	actress		la proyeccionista	16	projectionist
el decorado	4	set		el cine/el teatro	17	movie theater
las alas	5	wings		la pantalla	18	screen
las cortinas	6	curtain		el acomodador	19	usherette
el reflector	7	spotlight		los asientos	20	seats
el teatro	8	theater		el pasillo	21	aisle
la galería	9	gallery				
el palco/el balcón	10	balcony		La Biblioteca	**C.**	**The Library**
la planta baja	11	orchestra		la bibliotecaria	22	librarian
la platea	12	(orchestra) pit		el fichero	23	card catalog
las candilejas	13	footlights		el escritorio	24	desk
				el estante de libros/el librero	25	bookshelf

la botella de cerveza	1	**(beer) bottle**	
la tapa/la corcholata	2	**bottle top**	
la jarra/el tarro	3	**stein/mug**	
la lata de cerveza	4	**(beer) can**	
los fósforos/los cerillos	5	**matchbook**	
el fósforo/el cerillo	6	**match**	
el destapador de botellas	7	**bottle opener**	
el cigarillo/el cigarro	8	**cigarette**	
la ceniza	9	**ash**	
el cenicero	10	**ashtray**	
el sacacorchos	11	**corkscrew**	
el papote/la paja/el sorbeto	12	**straw**	
el refresco	13	**soft drink**	
el encendedor	14	**lighter**	
la barra/el mostrador	15	**bar**	
la cerveza de barril	16	**draft beer**	
la bebida/el licor	17	**hard liquor**	

la cantinera	18	**cocktail waitress**
el cantinero	19	**bartender**
la llave de cerveza	20	**tap**
el taburete	21	**(bar)stool**
el mozo/el mesero/el camarero	22	**waiter**
el cliente	23	**customer**
el menú/la carta	24	**menu**
la botella de vino	25	**bottle of wine**
el corcho	26	**cork**
el vaso de vino	27	**(wine) glass**
el salero	28	**saltshaker**
el moledor de pimienta	29	**pepper mill**
el pimentero	30	**pepper shaker**
el mantel	31	**tablecloth**
la servilleta	32	**napkin**
la cuenta	33	**check**
la medida para las bebidas	34	**jigger**

El Ajedrez y Las Damas	**A.**	**Chess and Checkers**
el juego de ajedrez	1	chess set
el tablero	2	board
el peón	3	pawn
la torre	4	castle/rook
el caballo	5	knight
el alfil	6	bishop
la reina	7	queen
el rey	8	king
el juego de damas	9	checkers

La Baraja/Las Cartas	**B.**	**Cards**
el juego de barajas	10	(deck of) cards
la jota de trébol	11	jack of clubs
la reina de diamantes	12	queen of diamonds
el rey de corazones	13	king of hearts
el as de espadas	14	ace of spades

La Lectura	**C.**	**Reading**
el libro	15	book
la pasta	16	cover
la portada	17	(dust) jacket
el lomo	18	spine
la página	19	page
la ilustración	20	illustration
el texto	21	text

La Fotografía	**D.**	**Photography**
la fotografía/la foto	22	photograph/photo
el negativo	23	negative
el rollo de película	24	(roll of) film
la cámara	25	camera
los lentes	26	lens
la pantalla	27	screen
el trípode	28	stand
el proyector	29	(slide) projector
la diapositiva/ la transparencia	30	slide

la máquina de coser	1	sewing machine	los volantes	14	ruffle
la cinta métrica/el centímetro	2	tape	el botón	15	button
la costura	3	seam	el ojal	16	buttonhole
la bastilla/el dobladillo/ el ruedo	4	hem	la puntada	17	stitch
			la aguja de tejer	18	knitting needle
el dedal	5	thimble	la lana	19	wool
la aguja	6	needle	el patrón/el modelo	20	pattern
el elástico	7	elastic	el tejido	21	knitting
el carrete de hilo	8	(spool of) thread	el cierre	22	zipper
el encaje	9	lace	el macho y la hembra/ el broche	23	hook and eye
el alfiler de seguridad	10	safety pin			
el pliegue/el plisado/ el tableado	11	pleat	el listón/la cinta	24	ribbon
			la cinta para medir	25	tape measure
el alfiler	12	(common)/(straight) pin	las tijeras	26	scissors
			el broche de presión	27	snap
la tela	13	material/cloth			

la peluquera	1	hairdresser	la mecanógrafa	9	typist
el carnicero	2	butcher	la modista/la costurera	10	dressmaker
el carpintero	3	carpenter	la mesera/la camarera	11	waitress
el empleado de banco	4	bank teller	el conductor/el chofer	12	truck driver
el mecánico	5	mechanic	el payaso	13	clown
el estibador	6	longshoreman	el portero	14	redcap/porter
el minero	7	miner	el locutor	15	announcer
la pintora/el artista	8	artist			

el vendedor de frutas	1	**fruit seller**	el vendedor/el dependiente	9	**salesman**
el electricista	2	**electrician**	la enfermera	10	**nurse**
el jardinero	3	**gardener**	la maestra	11	**teacher**
el fotógrafo	4	**photographer**	el soldado	12	**soldier**
la florista	5	**florist**	el policía	13	**policeman**
el barbero/el peluquero	6	**barber**	el oculista	14	**optician**
el panadero	7	**baker**	el marinero	15	**sailor**
el médico/el doctor	8	**doctor**			

el caballo	1	horse		el cachorro/el perrito	14	puppy
el potrillo	2	foal		el gato	15	cat
el cerdo/el cochino/el puerco/	3	pig		el gatito	16	kitten
el lechón				la pezuña/la pata	17	paw
el hocico	4	snout		el ratón	18	mouse
la llama	5	llama		la ardilla	19	squirrel
el camello	6	camel		el conejo	20	rabbit
la joroba	7	hump		el bigote	21	whisker
el búfalo	8	buffalo		la rata	22	rat
el cuerno	9	horn		la cola	23	tail
el burro	10	donkey		el zorro	24	fox
el reno/el tarado	11	reindeer		el murciélago	25	bat
el cuerno/la asta	12	antler		el erizo	26	hedgehog
el perro	13	dog				

la ballena	1	whale
la aleta	2	tail/fluke
el delfín	3	dolphin
la aleta	4	fin
el antílope	5	antelope
el canguro	6	kangaroo
la bolsa	7	pouch
el oso	8	bear
la foca	9	seal
la aleta	10	flipper
el lobo	11	wolf
el mandril	12	baboon
el mono	13	monkey
el gorila	14	gorilla
la jirafa	15	giraffe
el león	16	lion
la melena	17	mane
el leopardo	18	leopard
el tigre	19	tiger
el hipopótamo	20	hippopotamus
el elefante	21	elephant
la trompa	22	trunk
el colmillo	23	tusk
la cebra	24	zebra
el rinoceronte	25	rhinoceros
el cuerno	26	horn

Los Peces y Otros Animales		Fish and Other Animals
el tiburón	1	shark
la aleta	2	fin
el pez espada	3	swordfish
el salmón	4	salmon
la agalla	5	gill
el arenque	6	herring
la cola	7	tail
el hocico	8	snout
las escamas	9	scales
la anguila	10	eel
la medusa/la aguamala	11	jellyfish
la langosta de mar	12	lobster
el caracol	13	snail
el caparazón/la concha	14	shell
el pez dorado	15	sunfish
la ostra/el ostión	16	oyster
el cangrejo	17	crab
la pinza	18	pincer/claw
la babosa	19	slug
el sapo	20	frog
el gusano	21	worm
el cienpiés	22	centipede
el pulpo	23	octopus
el tentáculo	24	tentacle
la araña	25	spider
la tela de araña/la telaraña	26	(spider) web
el escorpión/el alacrán	27	scorpion

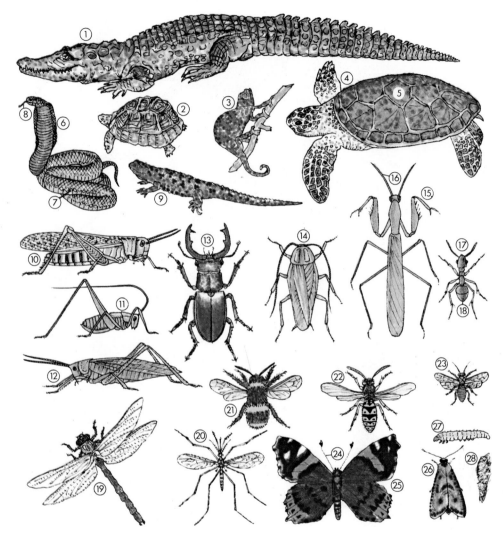

Los Reptiles	**Reptiles**	
el cocodrilo	1	crocodile
la tortuga	2	tortoise
el camaleón	3	chameleon
la tortuga	4	turtle
la coraza	5	shell
la culebra/la serpiente	6	snake
las escamas	7	scale
la lengua	8	tongue
la lagartija	9	lizard

Los Insectos	**Insects**	
la langosta	10	locust
el grillo	11	cricket
el saltamontes/el chapulín	12	grasshopper

el escarabajo	13	beetle
la cucaracha	14	cockroach
el mantis	15	mantis
la antena	16	feeler
la hormiga	17	ant
el abdomen	18	abdomen
la libélula	19	dragonfly
el mosquito	20	mosquito
la abeja	21	bee
la avispa	22	wasp
la mosca	23	fly
la antena	24	antenna
la mariposa	25	butterfly
la polilla	26	moth
la oruga	27	caterpillar
la crisálida	28	cocoon

Los Pájaros	**Birds**		el cisne	17	swan
el avestruz	1	ostrich	el canario	18	canary
el águila	2	eagle	el pico de ave	19	bill
la garra	3	claw	el loro/la cotorra	20	parrot
el pico	4	beak	la gaviota	21	(sea)gull
las plumas	5	feathers	la golondrina	22	swallow
el halcón/el gavilán	6	hawk	el ala	23	wing
la lechuza	7	owl	la paloma torcaz	24	dove
el flamingo/el flamenco	8	flamingo	el ganso	25	goose
la pata con membrana entre los dedos	9	webbed foot	el periquito	26	parakeet
			el colibrí/el chupaflor	27	hummingbird
el buitre	10	vulture	el gorrión	28	sparrow
el pavo real	11	peacock	el nido	29	nest
la cresta	12	crest	el martín pescador	30	kingfisher
el pingüino	13	penguin	la paloma/el pichón	31	pigeon
el faisán	14	pheasant	el mirlo	32	blackbird
la garza	15	heron	el cuervo	33	crow
el pavo/el guajalote	16	turkey			

Las Frutas		Fruit
la manzana	1	apple
el tallo	2	stalk
la piel/la cáscara	3	skin
la semilla	4	core
el plátano/el guineo	5	banana
la cáscara	6	peel
la cereza	7	cherry
la pepa/la semilla	8	pit/stone
el coco	9	coconut
el dátil	10	date
el cacahuete/el maní	11	peanut
las uvas	12	grapes
la parra	13	vine
el limón	14	lemon
el mango	15	mango
la naranja/la china	16	orange
los gajos/los tajos	17	sections
la corteza/la cáscara	18	peel/rind
el durazno/el melocotón	19	peach
la pepa/la semilla	20	pit/pip/stone
la fresa	21	strawberry
la pera	22	pear
la ciruela	23	plum
la piña/la ananá	24	pineapple
la papaya/la lechosa	25	papaya
la litchi	26	litchi
la nuez	27	walnut
la almendra	28	nutmeat
el higo	29	fig
la toronja/el pomelo	30	grapefruit
el cactus/el nopal	31	cactus
el helecho	32	fern
la fronda	33	frond

Las Legumbres	Vegetables		Las Flores	Flowers
el frijol/la habichuela	1	bean	el narciso	17 daffodil
el tallo	2	stalk	la margarita	18 daisy
el chícharo	3	pea	la rosa	19 rose
la vaina	4	pod	el pétalo	20 petal
la zanahoria	5	carrot	la orquídea	21 orchid
la papa	6	potato	el tulipán	22 tulip
la calabaza	7	squash	el tallo	23 stem
el pepino/el pepinillo	8	cucumber	el hibisco/la amapola	24 hibiscus
el betabel/la remolacha	9	beet	el capullo	25 bud
la coliflor	10	cauliflower	el lirio acuático	26 waterlily
la col/el repollo	11	cabbage	el girasol/el mirasol	27 sunflower
la lechuga	12	lettuce	las semillas	28 seeds
la cebolla	13	onion		
el hongo/la seta	14	mushroom		
el jitomate/el tomate	15	tomato		
la berenjena	16	eggplant		

la mazorca de maíz	1	(ear of) corn
el trigo	2	wheat
la aceituna	3	olive
el grano de cacao	4	cocoa bean
el grano de café	5	coffee berry
el algodón	6	cotton
el arroz	7	rice
el té	8	tea
la caña de azúcar	9	sugar cane
el roble/el encino	10	oak tree
las raíces	11	roots
el tronco	12	trunk

la rama	13	branch/bough
la ramita	14	twig
la hoja	15	leaf
la bellota	16	acorn
la corteza	17	bark
el leño/el palo	18	log
la palmera/la palma	19	palm
el abeto/el pino	20	fir
la piña/el cono	21	(pine)cone
las agujas	22	(pine) needles
el cedro	23	cedar
el sauce	24	willow

soplar	1	blow	
romper	2	break	
cargar / llevar	3	carry	
coger / tomar	4	catch	
escalar / subir	5	climb	
gatear	6	crawl	
llorar	7	cry / weep	
cortar	8	cut	
bailar / danzar	9	dance	
cavar / excavar	10	dig	
zambullirse	11	dive	
dibujar	12	draw	
beber / tomar	13	drink	

soñar	14	dream	
conducir / manejar	15	drive	
ahogarse	16	drown	
comer	17	eat	
caerse	18	fall	
pelear	19	fight	
volar	20	fly	
saltar / brincar	21	jump / leap	
patear	22	kick	
arrodillarse	23	kneel	
reírse	24	laugh	
lamer	25	lick	

escuchar/oir	1	listen
abrir	2	open
estar acostado	3	lie
pintar	4	paint
halar	5	pull
empujar	6	push
leer	7	read
cabalgar/montar a caballo	8	ride
correr	9	run
navegar	10	sail
coser	11	sew
disparar	12	shoot
cerrar	13	shut

cantar	14	sing
sentar(se)	15	sit
sonreír	16	smile
parar(se)	17	stand
mover/revolver	18	stir
barrer	19	sweep
nadar	20	swim
desgarrar/romper	21	tear
tocar	22	touch
atar/ligar	23	tie
caminar	24	walk
lavar	25	wash

despedir/agitar	1	wave	pasar/dejar atrás	13	pass
escribir	2	write	fruncir el ceño	14	frown
dar cuerda	3	wind	poner	15	put
doblar	4	bend	hilar/retorcer/dar vuelta	16	spin
pegar/golpear	5	hit/beat	aplaudir	17	clap
abrazar	6	hug	planchar	18	iron
besar	7	kiss	dormir	19	sleep
levantar	8	pick	sostener/agarrar	20	hold
tirar	9	throw	escribir a máquina	21	type
doblar/torcer/dar vuelta	10	turn	hervir	22	boil
dar	11	give	cortar (leña)	23	chop
peinar	12	comb			

la caja de cartón	1	carton	el safacón/el bote de basura	12	trash can
la bolsa de papel	2	paper bag/sack	el barril	13	barrel
la bolsa plástica	3	plastic garden bag	la canasta/el cesto	14	basket
la bolsa para emparedados	4	sandwich bag	la caja	15	box
la botella	5	bottle	el baúl	16	trunk
el jarro	6	jar	la caja de embalaje	17	crate
la lata	7	can	la bolsa de compras	18	shopping bag
el vaso de papel	8	paper cup	la maleta/la valija	19	suitcase
el termo	9	thermos	el maletín	20	carry-on case
la envoltura plástica	10	plastic wrap	la cartera/la billetera	21	wallet
el papel de aluminio	11	aluminum foil			

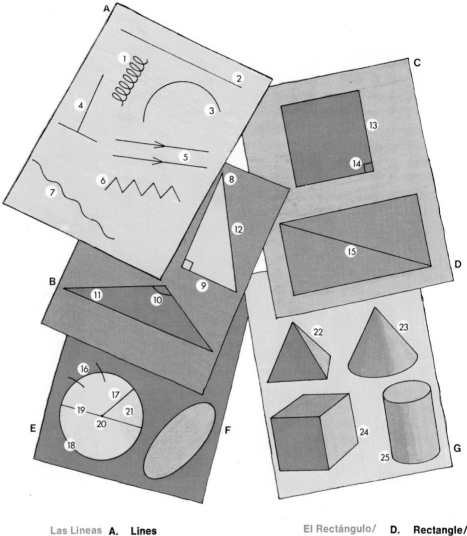

Las Líneas	**A.**	**Lines**
la línea espiral	1	spiral
la línea recta	2	straight line
la línea curva	3	curve
la línea perpendicular	4	perpendicular line
las líneas paralelas	5	parallel lines
la línea zig-zag	6	zigzag
la línea curva	7	wavy line
Los Triángulos	**B.**	**Triangles**
el ápice	8	apex
la base	9	base
el ángulo obtuso	10	obtuse angle
el ángulo agudo	11	acute angle
la hipotenusa	12	hypotenuse
Los Cuadriláteros	**C.**	**Square**
el lado	13	side
el ángulo derecho/recto	14	right angle

El Rectángulo/	**D.**	**Rectangle/Oblong**
El Cuadrilongo		
la diagonal	15	diagonal
Los Círculos	**E.**	**Circle**
el arco	16	arc
el radio	17	radius
la circunferencia	18	circumference
el diámetro	19	diameter
el centro	20	center
la sección	21	section
El Ovalo/La Elipse	**F.**	**Oval/Ellipse**
Las Figuras Sólidas	**G.**	**Solid Figures**
la pirámide	22	pyramid
el cono	23	cone
el cubo	24	cube
el cilindro	25	cylinder

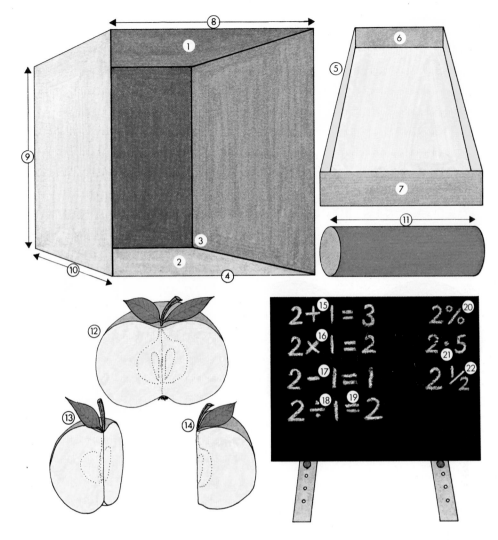

On the blackboard:

$$2 + 1 = 3 \qquad 2\%$$
$$2 \times 1 = 2 \qquad 2 \cdot 5$$
$$2 - 1 = 1 \qquad 2\tfrac{1}{2}$$
$$2 \div 1 = 2$$

la parte de arriba	1	**top**	una mitad	12	**a half**
la parte de abajo	2	**bottom**	un tercio/una tercera parte	13	**a third**
la esquina	3	**corner**	un cuarto/una cuarta parte	14	**a quarter**
el borde	4	**edge**	más	15	**plus**
el lado	5	**side**	multiplicado por	16	**multiplied by**
la espalda	6	**back**	menos	17	**minus**
el frente	7	**front**	dividido por	18	**divided by**
el ancho	8	**width**	igual/iguales	19	**equals**
la altura	9	**height**	el por ciento/el porcentaje	20	**per cent**
la profundidad	10	**depth**	el punto decimal	21	**decimal point**
el largo	11	**length**	la fracción	22	**fraction**

La Hora		**The Time**
el minutero	1	minute hand
la manecilla de la hora	2	hour hand
el segundero	3	second hand
la carátula/la faz (del reloj)	4	clock face
las nueve en punto	5	9:00: nine o'clock
las nueve y diez	6	9:10: ten after nine/nine-ten
las nueve y cuarto/las nueve y quince	7	9:15: a quarter after nine/nine-fifteen
las nueve y media/las nueve y treinta	8	9:30: nine-thirty
las diez menos cuarto/las nueve y cuarenta y cinco	9	9:45: a quarter of ten/nine forty-five
las diez menos diez/las nueve cincuenta	10	9:50: ten of ten/nine-fifty

La Fecha		**The Date**
el calendario	11	calendar
La fecha de hoy es miércoles dieciséis de julio de mil novecientos ochenta: 16 de julio de 1980 o 16/7/1980.		Today's date is Wednesday the sixteenth of July/July sixteenth nineteen eighty: July 16, 1980 or 7/16/80.

La Temperatura		**The Temperature**
el termómetro	12	thermometer
La temperatura es de 18 grados centígrados o 65 grados Farenheit.		The temperature is 18 degrees Centigrade (18°C) or 65 degrees Fahrenheit (65°F).

Alan Smith   Ann Brown

Ben Jones   Bob Smith   Betty Smith   Brenda Taylor

Cliff Jones   Carol Jones   Colin Smith

Alan y Ana son **marido** y **mujer**.	1	Alan and Ann are **husband** and **wife.**
Sus **hijos** son Betty y Bob.	2	Their **children** are Betty and Bob.
Su **hija** es Betty y su **hijo** es Bob.	3	Their **daughter** is Betty and their **son** is Bob.
Alan es el **padre** de Bob y Ana es la **madre** de Bob.	4	Alan is Bob's **father** and Ann is Bob's **mother.**
Betty es la **hermana** de Bob y Bob es el **hermano** de Betty.	5	Betty is Bob's **sister** and Bob is Betty's **brother.**
Alan es el **suegro** de Ben y Ana es su **suegra**.	6	Alan is Ben's **father-in-law** and Ann is his **mother-in-law.**
Ben es el **yerno** y Brenda la **nuera** de Alan y Ana.	7	Ben is Alan and Ann's **son-in-law** and Brenda is their **daughter-in-law.**
Ben es el **hermano político/cuñado** de Bob y Brenda es la **hermana política/cuñada** de Betty.	8	Ben is Bob's **brother-in-law** and Brenda is Betty's **sister-in-law.**
Colin es el **primo** de Cliff y de Carol.	9	Colin is Cliff and Carol's **cousin.**
Betty es la **tía** de Colin y Ben es su **tío**.	10	Betty is Colin's **aunt** and Ben is his **uncle.**
Colin es el **sobrino** de Betty y Carol es la **sobrina** de Bob.	11	Colin is Betty's **nephew** and Carol is Bob's **niece.**
Cliff es el **nieto** y Carol es la **nieta** de Ana y Alan.	12	Cliff is Ann and Alan's **grandson** and Carol is their **granddaughter.**

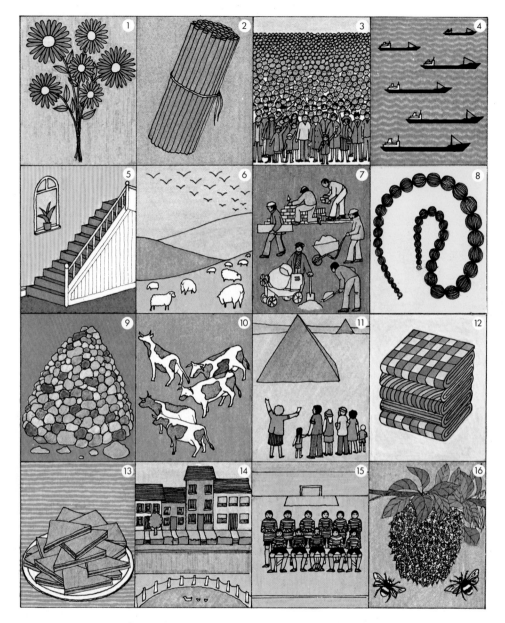

el ramo (de flores)	**1**	**bunch (of flowers)**	
el haz/el manojo (de varas)	**2**	**bundle (of sticks)**	
la muchedumbre	**3**	**crowd (of people)**	
la flota (de barcos)	**4**	**fleet (of ships)**	
el tramo (de escaleras)	**5**	**flight (of stairs)**	
la manada (de ovejas)/	**6**	**flock (of sheep**	
la bandada (de pájaros)		**or birds)**	
la cuadrilla (de trabajadores)	**7**	**gang (of workmen)**	
el collar	**8**	**string (of beads)**	

el montón (de piedras)	**9**	**pile (of stones)**
el rebaño (de vacas)	**10**	**herd (of cattle)**
el grupo (de turistas)	**11**	**group (of tourists)**
la pila/el montón	**12**	**pile (of blankets)**
(de frazadas)		
el plato (de bocadillos)	**13**	**plate (of sandwich**
la hilera (de casas)	**14**	**row (of houses)**
el equipo (de jugadores)	**15**	**team (of players)**
el enjambre (de abejas)	**16**	**swarm (of bees)**

el ovillo (de hilo, lana)	1	ball (of string/twine)	
la caja (de galletas)	2	box (of cookies)	
la barra (de jabón)	3	bar (of soap)	
el vaso (de leche)	4	glass (of milk)	
la botella (de vino)	5	bottle (of wine)	
el pan	6	loaf (of bread)	
el terrón (de azúcar)	7	lump (of sugar)	
el pedazo (de bizcocho)	8	piece (of cake)	

el carrete (de hilo)	9	spool (of thread)	
la caja (de cerillos/ fósforos)	10	box (of matches)	
el paquete (de cigarrillos/ cigarros)		pack (of cigarettes)	
la taza de café	11	cup (of coffee)	
el rollo (de papel)	12	roll (of paper)	
el tubo (de dentrífico)	13	tube (of toothpaste)	
el tazón (de sopa)	14	bowl (of soup)	

a) grande	**1**	a) big/large	
b) pequeño/chico		b) little/small	
a) sin punta/romo/boto	**2**	a) blunt	
b) afilado/cortante		b) sharp	
a) limpio	**3**	a) clean	
b) sucio		b) dirty	
a) cerrado	**4**	a) closed/shut	
b) abierto		b) open	
a) torcido	**5**	a) crooked	
b) derecho		b) straight	
a) poco profundo	**6**	a) shallow	
b) profundo		b) deep	
a) mojado	**7**	a) wet	
b) seco		b) dry	
a) vacío	**8**	a) empty	
b) lleno		b) full	

a) rápido	**9**	a) fast	
b) lento		b) slow	
a) gordo	**10**	a) fat	
b) delgado		b) thin	
a) feliz	**11**	a) happy	
b) triste		b) sad	
a) fácil	**12**	a) easy	
b) difícil/duro		b) difficult/hard	
a) suave	**13**	a) soft	
b) duro		b) hard	
a) alto	**14**	a) high	
b) bajo		b) low	
a) caliente	**15**	a) hot	
b) frío		b) cold	
a) largo	**16**	a) long	
b) corto		b) short	

a) angosto/estrecho	**1**	a) **narrow**
b) ancho		b) **wide**
a) joven	**2**	a) **young**
b) viejo		b) **old**
a) nuevo	**3**	a) **new**
b) viejo		b) **old**
a) calmado	**4**	a) **calm**
b) borrascoso		b) **rough**
a) áspero	**5**	a) **rough**
b) liso/suave		b) **smooth**
a) fuerte	**6**	a) **strong**
b) débil		b) **weak**
a) ordenado	**7**	a) **neat**
b) desordenado		b) **sloppy/messy**
a) bueno	**8**	a) **good**
b) malo		b) **bad**

a) bonito/hermoso	**9**	a) **pretty/beautiful**
b) feo		b) **ugly**
a) primero	**10**	a) **first**
b) último		b) **last**
a) claro	**11**	a) **light**
b) oscuro		b) **dark**
a) liviano	**12**	a) **light**
b) pesado		b) **heavy**
a) ruidoso	**13**	a) **loud**
b) suave		b) **soft**
a) sólido	**14**	a) **solid**
b) hueco		b) **hollow**
a) grueso	**15**	a) **thick**
b) delgado		b) **thin**
a) suelto	**16**	a) **loose**
b) ajustado/apretado		b) **tight**

afuera de la habitación	1	**outside** the room
a través de la puerta	2	**through** the door
bajo el cuadro	3	**below** the picture
bajando por la pared	4	**down** the wall
subiendo por la pared	5	**up** the wall
alrededor del cuello	6	**around** the neck
frente a la silla	7	**in front of** the chair
contra la pared	8	**against** the wall
dentro del cajón	9	**into** the drawer
en el cajón	10	**in/inside** the drawe
afuera del cajón	11	**out of** the drawer
sobre la mesa	12	**on** the table
encima de la mesa	13	**on to/onto** the table
al lado de/junto a la mesa	14	**beside/next to** the table
cerca de la silla	15	**by/near** the chair
detrás de la silla	16	**behind** the chair
debajo/abajo de la mesa	17	**under/underneath/ beneath** the table

encima de los árboles	1	**above** the trees	cruzando/**sobre** la carretera	7	**across/on** the road
más allá del puente	2	**beyond** the bridge	**en** la esquina	8	**at** the corner
de la playa	3	**from** the beach	**a lo largo de** la carretera	9	**along** the road
a la playa	4	**to** the beach	**hacia** el puente	10	**toward** the bridge
entre los árboles	5	**among** the trees	**lejos del** puente	11	**away from** the bridge
fuera de la carretera	6	**off** the road	**entre** los automóviles	12	**between** the cars

There is both an English Index and a Spanish Index in this text. The Spanish Index lists each Spanish word used in the dictionary with its page and item number. The English Index includes a pronunciation guide and a phonemic transcription for each English word in the book.

There are two numbers after each word in each index. The first number refers to the page where the word is listed. The second number refers to the item number of the word.

For example: abdomen /ǽbdəmən/59/18 means that the word "abdomen" is the eighteenth item on page 59.

Hay un índice de Inglés y uno de Español en este libro. El índice de Español incluye cada palabra española que se encuentra en el libro. El índice de Inglés incluye una guía de pronunciación y una transcripción fonémica para cada palabra inglesa que se encuentra en el libro.

Después de cada palabra hay dos números. El primer número indica la página donde se encuentra la palabra. El segundo se refiere al número de la palabra en sí.

Por ejemplo: **abdomen** /ǽbdəmən/**59**/18 quiere decir que esta palabra es la dieciochava palabra en la página 59.

Vowels
/a/ as in calm /kam/
/æ/ as in hat /hæt/
/e/ as in wait /wet/
/ɛ/ as in wet /wɛt/

/ə/ as in butter /bə́tər/
/i/ as in leak /lik/
/ɪ/ as in lick /lɪk/
/o/ as in note /not/

/ɔ/ as in cough /kɔf/
/u/ as in broom /brum/
/ʊ/ as in book /bʊk/

Consonants
/b/ as in base /bes/
/č/ as in chip /čɪp/
/d/ as in dog /dɔg/
/ð/ as in this /ðɪs/
/f/ as in five /faɪv/
/g/ as in girl /gərl/
/h/ as in hand /hænd/
/ǰ/ as in jacket /ǰǽkɪt/

/k/ as in cat /kæt/
/l/ as in lick /lɪk/
/m/ as in man /mæn/
/n/ as in win /wɪn/
/ŋ/ as in sing /sɪŋ/
/p/ as in pin /pɪn/
/r/ as in red /rɛd/
/s/ as in sip /sɪp/

/š/ as in ship /šɪp/
/t/ as in tin /tɪn/
/θ/ as in thin /θɪn/
/v/ as in vase /ves/
/w/ as in waist /west/
/y/ as in yard / yard/
/z/ as in zebra /zíbrə/
/ž/ as in measure /méžər/

/´/ over a vowel shows that the vowel has strong stress, eg. *address* /ǽdrɛs/ (noun), /ədrǽs/ (verb); *present* /prézɪnt/ (noun), /prɪzént/ (verb).

NDEX

bdomen /ǽbdəmən/**59**/18
bove /əbÁv/**77**/1
ccelerator /ıkséləretər/**38**/18; **40**/32
ccused /əkyúzd/**16**/20
ce of spades /es-əv-spédz/**52**/14
corn /ékɔrn/**63**/16
cross /əkrɔ́s/**77**/7
ctor /ǽktər/**50**/2
ctress /ǽktrıs/**50**/3
cute angle /əkyút-ǽŋgəl/**68**/11
dding machine /ǽdıŋ-məšin/**21**/8
ddress /ədrés/**22**/11
djective /ǽjıktıv/**74–75**
erial /ériəl/**26**/19; **38**/9
erogram /ǽrogram/**22**/7
frica /ǽfrıkə/**6**/4
gainst /əgénst/**76**/8
ir /ær/**44**
ircraft-carrier /ǽr-kræft-kæriər/**45**/18
air-Force /ǽr-fɔrs/**45**
irplane /ǽr-plen/**44**/9
ir-pump /ǽr-pəmp/**39**/9
irliner /ǽr-laınər/**44**/9
irmail envelope/ǽrmel-ɛnvəlop/**22**/10
irport /ær-pɔrt/**44**
isle /aıl/**50**/21
larm-clock /əlárm-klak/**32**/25
long /əlɔ́ŋ/**77**/9
lps /ælps/**7**/38
luminum foil /əlúmınəm-fɔ́ıl/**67**/11
mazon /ǽməzan/**7**/46
mbulance /ǽmbyuləns/**39**/15; **47**/24
mong /əmɔ́ŋ/**77**/5
mplifier /ǽmplıfaıər/**29**/18; **49**/27
nchor /ǽŋkər/**42**/11
ndes /ǽndiz/**7**/37
nimal /ǽnəməl/**56–60**
nkle /ǽŋkəl/**8**/36
nnouncer /ənáunsər/**54**/15
nt /ænt/**59**/17
ntarctica /æntárktıkə/**6**/7
ntarctic Circle /æntárktık-sárkəl/**5**/6
ntelope /ǽtəlop/**57**/5
ntenna /ænténə/**26**/19; **38**/9
ntler /ǽntlər/**56**/12
partment house /əpártmənt-haus/**15**/18
pex /épɛks/**68**/8
pple /ǽpəl/**61**/1
rabian Desert /ərébiən-dézərt/**7**/43
rabian Sea /ərébiən-sí/**6**/27
rc /ark/**68**/16
rctic /árktık/**6**/8
rctic Circle /árktık-sárkəl/**5**/2
rm /arm/**8**/21
rmchair /árm-čɛr/**29**/11
rmpit /ármpıt/**8**/20
rmy /ármi/**45**
round /əraúnd/**76**/6
rtery /ártəri/**9**/30
rtist /ártıst/**54**/8
sh /æš/**51**/9
shtray /ǽštre/**29**/29; **51**/10
sia /éžə/**6**/5
stronaut /ǽstrənɔt/**4**/20
t /æt/**77**/8
ttendant /əténdənt/**39**/10
unt /ænt/**71**/10
ustralia /ɔstrélyə/**6**/6
way from /əwé-frəm/**77**/11
xe /æks/**24**/6

aboon /bæbún/**57**/13
aby /bébi/**32**
aby carriage /bébi-kærıj/**15**/17
abypowder /bébi-paudər/**32**/37
ack /bæk/**8**/15; **69**/6
ackboard /bæk-bɔrd/**46**/16
ackbone /bæk-bon/**8**/6
ackpack /bæk-pæk/**35**/4
ad /bæd/**75**/8
ag /bæg/**13**/4; **20**/6
aggage /bǽgıj/**44**/4
ait /bet/**48**/22

baker /békər/**55**/7
balcony /bǽlkəni/**26**/4; **50**/10
ball /bɔl/**46**/17; **48**/28; **73**/1
ball of string /bɔ́l-əv-strıŋ/**73**/1
ball of twine /bɔ́l-əv-twáın/**73**/1
Baltic Sea /báltık-sí/**6**/21
banana /bənǽnə/**61**/5
bandage /bǽndıj/**17**/27
banister /bǽnıstər/**28**/13
bank teller /bǽŋk-telər/**54**/4
bar /bar/**16**/16; **51**; **51**/15; **73**/2
barber /bárbər/**55**/6
barge /bárj/**43**/16
bark /bark/**63**/17
barn /barn/**36**/4
barnyard /barnyard/**36**/6
barrel /bǽrəl/**45**/14; **67**/13
barrette /barét/**13**/13
barstool /bár-stul/**51**/21
bartender /bár-tendər/**51**/19
base /bes/**68**/9
baseball /bés-bɔl/**48**
basket /bǽskıt/**20**/7; **46**/15; **67**/14
basketball /bǽskıt-bɔl/**46**
bat /bæt/**48**/1; **56**/25
bathmat /bǽθ-mæt/**33**/25
bathing suit /béðıŋ-sut/**35**/36
bathing trunks /béðıŋ-trəŋks/**35**/20
bathrobe /bæθ-rob/**10**/1; **12**/21
bathroom /bǽθ-rum/**33**
bathroom scale /bǽθ-rum-skél/**33**/24
bath tub /bǽθ-təb/**33**/1
baton /bətán/**49**/11
batter /bǽtər/**48**/2
battery /bǽtəri/**38**/32
bay /be/**5**/8
Bay of Bengal /bé-əv-bɛŋɔ́l/**6**/28
bayonet /béyənɛt/**45**/3
beach /bič/**35**/11
beachball /bíčbɔl/**35**/26
beach towel /bíč-tauəl/**35**/14
beach umbrella /bíč-əmbrɛlə/**35**/12
beak /bik/**60**/4
beaker /bíkər/**19**/15
bean /bin/**62**/1
bear /bɛr/**57**/8
beard /bırd/**9**/11
beat /bit/**66**/5
beautiful /byútıfəl/**75**/9a
bed /bɛd/**32**/1
bedroom /bédrum/**32**
bedspread /béd-spred/**32**/7
bee /bi/**59**/21
beer bottle /bír-batəl/**51**/1
beer can /bír-kæn/**51**/4
beet /bit/**62**/9
beetle /bítəl/**59**/13
behind /bıhaínd/**76**/16
bell /bɛl/**17**/10; **40**/2
below /bıló/**76**/3
belt /bɛlt/**10**/16
bench /bɛnč/**19**/7
bend /bɛnd/**66**/4
beneath /bıníθ/**76**/17
Bering Sea /bérıŋ-sí/**7**/35
beside /bısáıd/**76**/14
between /bıtwín/**77**/12
beyond /biánd/**77**/2
bib /bıb/**32**/35
bicycle /báısıkəl/**14**/5; **40**/1
big /bıg/**74**/1a
bike /baık/**40**/1
bill /bıl/**60**/19
bills /bılz/**20**/24
bird /bərd/**60**
bishop /bíšəp/**52**/6
bit /bıt/**25**/6; **46**/6
blackbird /blǽkbərd/**60**/32
blackboard /blǽkbɔrd/**18**/2
Black Sea /blǽk-sí/**6**/23
bladder /blǽdər/**9**/28
blade /bled/**33**/14
blanket /blǽŋkət/**32**/6
blind /blaınd/**26**/15
blotter /blátər/**21**/4
blouse /blaus/**13**/6
blow /blo/**64**/1
blunt /blənt/**74**/2a
board /bɔrd/**23**/11; **52**/2

boardwalk /bɔ́rdwɔk/**35**/9
body /bádi/**8**
boil /bɔıl/**66**/22
bollard /bálərd/**42**/14
bolt /bolt/**25**/8; **28**/4
bomb /bam/**45**/24
bomber /bámər/**45**/23
book /buk/**18**/14; **52**/15
bookbag /búk-bæg/**18**/6
bookcase /búk-kes/**21**/24; **29**/16
bookshelf /búk-šelf/**50**/25
boot /but/**10**/18; **13**/3; **17**/6
bottle /bátəl/**32**/33; **51**/1; **67**/5
bottle of wine /batəl-əv-waín/**51**/25; **73**/5
bottle opener /bátəl-opınər/**30**/23; **51**/7
bottle top /bátəl-tap/**51**/2
bottom /bátəm/**69**/2
bough /báu/**63**/13
bow /báu/**43**/13; **49**/6
bowl /bol/**30**/35; **73**/14
bowl of soup /bɔ́l-əv-súp/**73**/14
box /baks/**67**/15; **73**/10
boxer /báksər/**46**/11
box of cookies /báks-əv-kúkiz/**73**/2
box of matches /báks-əv-mǽčız/**73**/10
box of tissues /báks-əv-tíšuz/**32**/23
boxing /báksıŋ/**46**
boxing glove /báksıŋ-gləv/**46**/12
boy /bɔ́ı/**10**
bra /bra/**12**/1
brace /bres/**25**/5
bracelet /bréslıt/**12**/8
brain /bren/**9**/21
brake /brek/**38**/22; **40**/14
brakeman /brekmən/**41**/10
branch /brænč/**27**/13; **63**/13
bread /bred/**20**/19
bread box /bréd-baks/**30**/15
break /brek/**64**/2
breastbone /brést-bon/**8**/4
brick /brık/**23**/8
bricklayer /brík-leər/**23**/2
bridge /brıj/**14**/12
bridle /bráıdəl/**46**/5
briefcase /bríf-kes/**11**/28
broiler /brɔ́ılər/**30**/3
broom /brum/**31**/2
brother /brɔ́ðər/**71**/5
brother-in-law /brɔ́ðər-ın-lɔ/**71**/8
brush /brəš/**12**/20
bucket /bákət/**31**/19; **35**/24
buckle /bákəl/**10**/17
bud /bad/**62**/25
buffalo /báfəlo/**56**/8
buffer /báfər/**41**/29
building /bíldıŋ/**23**
bulb /bálb/**31**/13
bull /bul/**36**/23
bullet /búlət/**45**/11
bulletin board /búlətın-bɔrd/**21**/10
bumper /bəmpər/**38**/6
bunch /bənč/**72**/1
bunch of flowers/bánč-əv-fláuərz/**72**/1
bundle /bándəl/**72**/2
bundle of sticks/bándəl-av-stíks/**72**/2
Bunsen burner /bánsən-bárnər/**19**/12
buoy /búı/**42**/13
burner /bárnər/**30**/4
bus /bəs/**15**/24; **39**/17
bush /buš/**27**/22
bus stop /bəs-stap/**15**/25
butcher /búčər/**54**/2
butterfly /bátər-flaı/**59**/25
buttocks /bátəks/**8**/19
button /bátən/**11**/26; **53**/15
button hole /bátən-hol/**53**/16
by /báı/**76**/15

cab /kæb/**40**/22
cabbage /kǽbıj/**62**/11
cabinet /kǽbınıt/**30**/6
cable /kébəl/**22**/17; **37**/4; **40**/4; **42**/15
cactus /kǽktəs/**61**/31
cake /kek/**20**/21
calculator /kǽlkyəletər/**21**/3
calendar /kǽləndər/**18**/20; **21**/17; **70**/11
calf /kæf/**8**/35; **36**/22
calm /kam/**75**/4a
camel /kǽməl/**56**/6

camera /kǽmrə/**52**/25
camping /kǽmpɪŋ/**35**
campstove /kǽmp-stov/**35**/5
camping stove /kǽmpɪŋ-stov/**35**/5
can /kæn/**30**/22; **51**/4; **67**/7
canary /kənǽri/**60**/18
canned food /kǽnd-fúd/**20**/16
canoe /kənú/**43**/9
can-opener /kǽn-opənər/**30**/21
cap /kæp/**46**/9
capsule /kǽpsəl/**4**/19
captain /kǽptən/**44**/5
car /kar/**15**/30; **38**; **39**/16
car radio /kár-redio/**38**/25
carbon paper /kárbən-pepər/**21**/20
card /kard/**52**/10
card catalog /kárd-kætələg/**50**/23
card file /kárd-faɪl/**21**/26
cardigan /kárdɪgən/**10**/9
cargo /kárgo/**42**/6
Caribbean Sea /kærɪbíən-si/**6**/18
carpenter /kárpɪntər/**54**/3
carpet /kárpɪt/**29**/3
carrot /kǽrət/**62**/5
carry /kǽri/**64**/3
carry on case /kǽri-an-kes/**67**/20
carton /kártən/**67**/1
cartridge /kártrɪj/**45**/11
cashier /kæšír/**20**/2
cash register /kǽš-rejɪstər/**20**/3
Caspian Sea /kǽspiən-sí/**6**/24
castle /kǽsəl/**52**/4
cat /kæt/**56**/15
catch /kæč/**64**/4
catcher /kǽčər/**48**/5
catcher's mask /kǽčərz-mæsk/**48**/6
caterpillar /kǽtərpɪlər/**59**/27
cauliflower /kálɪflauər/**62**/10
cedar /sídər/**63**/23
ceiling /sílɪŋ/**29**/1
cell /sɛl/**16**/15
cello /čɛlo/**49**/8
cement /sɪmént/**23**/16
cement mixer /sɪmént-mɪksər/**23**/21
centigrade /séntɪgred/**70**/12
centipede /séntɪpid/**58**/22
center /séntər/**47**/15; **68**/20
center fielder /séntər fíldər/**48**/16
chain /čen/**40**/18; **47**/20
chair /čɛr/**29**/13; **30**/27
chalk /čɔk/**18**/4
chameleon /kəmíliən/**59**/3
changing table /čénjɪŋ-tebəl/**32**/32
check /čɛk/**51**/33
checkers /čɛkərz/**52**; **52**/9
checkout counter /čɛkaut-kauntər/**20**/4
cheek /čik/**9**/5
cheese /čiz/**20**/9
cherry /čɛri/**61**/7
chess /čɛs/**52**
chess set /čɛs-sɛt/**52**/1
chest /čɛst/**8**/14
chest of drawers /čɛst-ə-drɔərz/**32**/16
chick /čɪk/**36**/35
chicken /číkɪn/**36**/33
children /čɪldrɪn/**71**/2
chimney /čímni/**26**/2
chin /čɪn/**9**/6
chisel /čɪzəl/**24**/4
choke /čok/**38**/15
chop /čap/**66**/23
cigarette /sígərɛt/**51**/8
circle /sárkəl/**39**/4; **68**
circumference /sərkámfrəns/**68**/18
city /síti/**14–15**
clap /klæp/**66**/17
clarinet /klærɪnét/**49**/1
claw /klɔ/**58**/18
clean /klin/**74**/3a
clerk /klərk/**20**/8
cliff /klɪf/**35**/6
climb /klaɪm/**64**/5
clip /klɪp/**12**/23
clock-face /klák-fes/**70**/4
closed /klozd/**74**/4a
closet /klázət/**32**/14
cloth /klɔθ/**53**/13
clothes /kloz/**10–13**
clothesline /klóz-laɪn/**27**/28

clothespin /klóz-pɪn/**27**/30
cloud /kláud/**27**/2
clown /kláun/**54**/13
clutch /kləč/**38**/20
coach /koč/**41**/4
coastline /kóst-laɪn/**5**/11
coal /kol/**37**/9
coat /kot/**11**/14; **13**/11
coatrack /kót-ræk/**28**/9
cockpit /kákpɪt/**45**/22
cockroach /kákroč/**59**/14
cocktail waitress /káktel-wetrɪs/**51**/18
cocoa bean /kóko-bin/**63**/4
coconut /kókənət/**61**/9
cocoon /kəkún/**59**/28
coffee berry /kɔ́fi-bɛri/**63**/5
coffee pot /kɔ́fi-pat/**30**/20
coffee table /kɔ́fi-tebəl/**29**/23
coin /kɔ́ɪn/**20**/25
cold /kold/**74**/15b
cold water faucet /kold-wɔtər-fɔsɪt/**33**/3
collar /kálər/**11**/2
collar bone /kálər-bon/**8**/2
comb /kom/**12**/19; **32**/22; **66**/12
combine (noun) /kámbaɪn/**36**/16
comet /kámət/**4**/1
common pin /kámən-pín/**53**/12
compact /kámpækt/**12**/12
compartment /kəmpártmɪnt/**41**/5
compass /kámpəs/**5**; **18**/11
conductor /kəndáktər/**41**/6; **49**/10
cone /kon/**63**/21; **68**/23
Congo /kángo/**7**/50
constellation /kánstəlésən/**4**/2
container /kənténər/**67**
continent /kántɪnənt/**6**
control panel /kəntról-pænəl/**45**/28
control tower /kəntról-tauər/**44**/20
convertible /kənvártəbəl/**38**/38
cookie /kúki/**20**/20
cooling tower /kúlɪŋ-tauər/**37**/8
Coral Sea /kɔ́rəl-sí/**6**/29
cord /kɔrd/**28**/21; **31**/12
core /kɔr/**61**/4
cork /kɔrk/**51**/26
corkscrew /kɔ́rk-skru/**51**/11
corn /kɔrn/**63**/1
corner /kɔ́rnər/**69**/3
cottage /kátɪj/**35**/8
cotton /kátən/**63**/6
couch /káuč/**29**/9
counter /káuntər/**22**/3; **30**/8
country /kántri/**34**
court /kɔrt/**48**/23
court of law /kɔrt-əv-lɔ́/**16**c
cousin /kázɪn/**71**/9
cover /kávər/**52**/16
cow /kau/**36**/7; **28**/1
cowshed /káu-šed/**36**/3
crab /kræb/**58**/17
crackers /krǽkərz/**20**/26
crane /kren/**23**/1; **42**/4
crashhelmet /kræš-hɛlmɪt/**40**/27
crate /kret/**67**/17
crawl /krɔl/**64**/6
crescent moon /krésənt-mún/**4**/11
crest /krɛst/**60**/12
crib /krɪb/**32**/26
cricket /kríkɪt/**59**/11
crocodile /krákədaɪl/**59**/1
crooked /krúkəd/**74**/5a
crossbar /krɔ́s-bar/**40**/15
crosswalk /krɔ́s-wɔk/**14**/2
crow /kro/**60**/33
crowd /kráud/**72**/3
crowd of people /kráud-əv-pipəl/**72**r
crutch /krəč/**17**/26
cry /krái/**64**/7
crystal /krístəl/**19**/17
cube /kyub/**68**/24
cucumber /kyúkəmbər/**62**/8
cuff /kəf/**11**/3; **18**
cuff links /káf-lɪŋks/**11**/25
cup /kəp/**30**/37; **73**/11
cup of coffee /kəp-əv-kɔfi/**73**/11
curb /kərb/**14**/8
curtain /kártən/**26**/14; **29**/7; **50**/6
curtain rod /kártən-rad/**33**/30
curve /kərv/**68**/3

cushion /kúšən/**29**/10
customer /kástəmər/**20**/5; **51**/23
customs /kástəmz/**44**/1
customs officer /kástəmz-ɔfɪsər/**44**/2
cut /kət/**64**/8
cylinder /sílɪndər/**68**/25
cylinder head /sílɪndər-hɛd/**38**/36
cymbal /símbəl/**49**/29

daffodil /dǽfədɪl/**62**/17
daisy /dézi/**62**/18
dam /dæm/**37**/2
dance /dæns/**64**/9
Danube /dǽnyub/**7**/47
dark /dark/**75**/11b
dashboard /dáš-bɔrd/**38**/12
date /det/**61**/10; **70**
daughter /dɔ́tər/**71**/3
daughter-in-law /dɔ́tər-ɪn-lɔ/**71**/7
decimal point /désɪməl-pɔ́ɪnt/**69**/21
deck /dɛk/**43**/19
deck chair /dɛ́k-čɛr/**35**/19
deck of cards /dɛ́k-əv-kárdz/**52**/10
deep /dip/**74**/6b
defense /difɛ́ns/**45**
defendant /difɛ́ndənt/**16**/20
defense attorney/difɛ́ns-ətárni/**16**/21
degree /dɪgrí/**70**/12
delta /dɛ́ltə/**5**/9
dental assistant /dɛ́ntəl-əsɪstənt/**17**/14
dentist /dɛ́ntɪst/**17**; **17**/16
dentist's chair /dɛ́ntɪsts-čɛr/**17**/15
depth /dɛpθ/**69**/10
derrick /dɛ́rɪk/**37**/10
deserts /dɛ́zərts/**7**
desk /dɛsk/**18**/7; **21**/1; **32**/15; **50**/24
detection /ditékšən/**16**
diagonal /daɪǽgənəl/**68**/15
dial /daɪl/**19**/5; **28**/20
diameter /daɪǽmətər/**68**/19
diaper /dáɪpər/**32**/36
difficult /dífɪkəlt/**74**/12b
dig /dɪg/**64**/10
dirty /dárti/**74**/3b
dish towel /dɪš-tauəl/**30**/25
dish washer /dɪš-wɔšər/**30**/24
display window /dɪsplé-windo/**15**/21
distributor /dɪstríbyutər/**38**/34
dive /daɪv/**64**/11
diverter /dɪvártər/**33**/7
divide by /dɪváɪd baɪ/**69**/18
dock /dak/**42**/12
doctor /dáktər/**17**/21; **55**/8
dog /dɔg/**56**/13
doll /dal/**32**/31
dolphin /dálfɪn/**57**/3
donkey /dɔ́ŋki/**56**/10
door /dɔr/**26**/7; **28**/1
doormat /dɔ́r-mæt/**26**/18; **28**/6
double bass /dábəl-bes/**49**/9
dove /dəv/**60**/24
down /dáun/**76**/4
downstairs /dáunstérz/**28**/15
dragonfly /drǽgən-flaɪ/**59**/19
drain /dren/**14**/10; **33**/5
drainpipe /drén-paɪp/**23**/9; **26**/17
drain plug /drén-pləg/**33**/6
draft beer /drǽft-bír/**51**/16
drape /drep/**29**/8
draw /drɔ/**64**/12
dream /drim/**64**/14
dress /drɛs/**13**/10
dressing table /drɛ́sɪŋ-tebəl/**32**/10
dressing table skirt /drɛ́sɪŋ-tebəl skərt/**32**/11
dressmaker /drɛ́s-mekər/**54**/10
drill /drɪl/**17**/17
drink /drɪŋk/**64**/13
drive /dráɪv/**64**/15
driver /dráɪvər/**40**/25
drown /dráun/**64**/16
drum /drám/**49**/30
dry /drái/**74**/7b
duck /dək/**36**/32
duckling /dáklɪŋ/**36**/31
dump truck /dámp-trək/**23**/22
dust brush /dást-brəš/**31**/6
dustcloth /dástklɔθ/**31**/7
dust jacket /dást-jækɪt/**52**/17
dust pan /dást-pæn/**31**/8

eagle /íɡəl/60/2
ear /ır/9/3
ear of corn /ír-əv-kórn/63/1
earring /ír-rıŋ/12/9
earth /ə́rθ/4/7
east /ist/5/16
East China Sea /íst-čáınə-sí/7/32
easy /ízi/74/12a
eat /it/64/17
eclipse /ıklíps/4/10
edge /ɛj/69/4
education /ɛjukéšən/18–19
eel /il/58/10
egg /ɛg/20/11
eggplant /ɛ́g-plænt/62/16
elastic /ılǽstık/53/7
elbow /ɛ́lbo/8/23
electric can opener /ılɛ́ktrık-kǽn-opənər/30/19
electric drill /ılɛ́ktrık-dríl/25/4
electric guitar /ılɛ́ktrık-gıtár/49/26
electrician /ılɛktríšən/55/7
elephant /ɛ́ləfənt/57/21
ellipse /ılíps/68
emergency brake /ımə́rjınsi-brek/38/19
empty /ɛ́mpti/74/8a
end table /ɛ́nd-tebəl/29/25
engine /ɛ́njın/38/31; 41/3
engineer /ɛnjınír/41/2
envelope /ɛ́nvəlop/21/11; 22/10, 15
equal /íkwəl/69/19
equator /ıkwétər/5/4
eraser /ırésər/18/3
estuary /ɛ́styuɛri/5/10
Europe /yɔ́rəp/6/3
excavator /ɛ́kskəvetər/23/20
exhaust /ıgzɔ́st/38/7; 40/35
expressway /ıksprés-we/39/1
extension cord /ıksténšən-kɔrd/24/10
eye /áı/9/1
eyeball /áı-bɔl/9/15
eyebrow /áı-brau/9/16
eyelash /áı-læš/9/18
eyelid /áı-lıd/9/17
eye shadow /áı-šædo/12/16

face /fes/9
ice cream /fes-krim/12/17
Fahrenheit /fǽrınhaıt/70/12
fall /fɔl/64/18
family /fǽmli/71
fare /fær/40/24
farm /farm/36
farmer /fármər/36/15
farm house /fárm-haus/36/7
fast /fæst/74/9a
fat /fæt/74/10a
father /fáðər/71/4
father-in-law /fáðər-ın-lɔ/71/6
feather /féðər/60/5
feeler /fílər/59/16
fence /fɛns/36/10
fern /fərn/61/32
ferry /féri/43/15
field /fild/34/13; 36/8; 47/6
field hockey /fíld-haki/46
fig /fıg/61/29
fight /faıt/64/19
fighter plane /fáıtər-plen/45/21
figure /fígyər/68
file /fáıl/21/18; 24/2
file cabinet /fáıl-kæbınıt/21/19
filing cabinet /fáılıŋ-kæbınıt/21/19
film /fılm/52/24
fin /fın/57/4; 58/2
finger /fíŋgər/8/30
finger-nail /fíŋgər-nel/8/31
fingerprint /fíŋgər-prınt/16/11
fir /fər/63/20
fire /fáıər/17; 17/12; 29/6
Fire Department /fáıər-dipartmənt/17
fire engine /fáıər-ɛnjın/17/7
fire escape /fáıər-ıskep/17/11
fire extinguisher /fáıər-ıkstıŋgwıšər/17/5
fire hose /fáıər-hoz/17/3
fire hydrant /fáıər-haıdrənt/17/4
fireman /fáıərmən/17/1
fireman's boot /faıərmənz-but/17/6
fireman's hat /fáıərmənz hæt/17/2

fireplace /fáıər-ples/29/4
fire truck /fáıər-trək/17/7
first /fərst/75/10a
first base /fərst-bés/48/9
first baseman /fərst-bésmən/48/10
fish /fıš/20/22; 58
fisherman /fíšərmən/48/18
fishing /fíšıŋ/48
fishing rod /fíšıŋ-rad/48/19
fist /fıst/8/26
flag /flæg/41/11
flamingo /fləmíŋgo/60/8
flap /flæp/22/16
flashlight /flǽš-laıt/16/9
flask /flæsk/19/16
fleet /flít/72/4
fleet of ships /flit-əv-šıps/72/4
flight /fláıt/72/5
flight attendant /fláıt-əténdənt/44/7, 8
flight of stairs /fláıt-əv-stǽrz/72/5
flipper /flípər/35/21; 57/10
flock /flak/72/6
flock of birds /flák-əv-bárdz/72/6
flock of sheep /flák-əv-šíp/72/6
floor /flɔr/28/7
florist /flɔ́rıst/55/5
flower /fláuər/27/20; 62
flower bed /fláuər-bed/27/21
flower pot /fláuər-pat/27/24
fluke /fluk/57/2
fly /fláı/59/23; 64/20
foal /fol/56/2
folding rule /fóldıŋ-rúl/24/12
foot /fut/8/37
football /fútbɔl/47; 47/1
footlights /fút-laıts/50/13
footpath /fút-pæθ/34/17
footprint /fút-prınt/16/12
footrest /fút-rest/40/37
forearm /fɔ́r-arm/8/24
forehead /fɔ́r-hɛd/9/8
forest /fɔ́rıst/34/9
fork /fork/30/33
forklift /fɔ́rk-lıft/42/17
foul line /fául-laın/48/14
foundations /faundéšənz/23/10
fox /faks/56/24
fraction /frǽkšən/69/22
freeway /frí-we/39/1
freezer /frízər/20/14
freight car /frét-kar/41/28
frog /frɔg/58/7
from /frəm/77/3
frond /frand/61/33
front /frənt/69/7
front door /frʌ́nt-dór/26/7
frown /fraun/66/14
fruit /fruit/20/17; 30/11; 61
fruit basket /frút-bæskıt/30/10
fruit seller /frút-sɛlər/55/1
fruit tree /frút-tri/36/11
frying pan /fráıŋ-pæn/30/14
full /ful/74/8b
full moon /fúl-mun/4/13
full back /fúl-bæk/47/10
furrow /fə́ro/36/20
fuselage /fyúsəlaž/44/10

galaxy /gǽləksi/4/3
gallery /gǽləri/50/9
game /gem/32/2
gang /gæŋ/72/7
gang of workmen /gǽŋ-əv-wórkmın/72/7
Ganges /gǽnjiz/7/52
gangway /gǽŋwe/42/10
garage /gəráž/26/6
garbage can /gárbıj-kæn/30/9
gardener /gárdnər/55/3
gas gauge /gǽs-gej/38/13
gas pump /gǽs-pəmp/39/8
gas station /gǽs-stešən/39/7
gas cap /gǽs-kæp/38/3
gate /get/27/16; 41/17
gateman /gét-mæn/41/16
gearshift /gír-šıft/38/21; 40/38
gill /gıl/58/5
giraffe /jərǽf/57/15
girl /gərl/12–13
give /gıv/66/11

glass /glæs/30/36; 33/18; 51/27; 73/4
glasses /glǽsız/11/23
glider /gláıdər/44/14
globe /glob/55
glove /glʌv/11/20; 48/7
glue /glu/18/13
goalpost /gól-post/47/4,22
goat /got/36/24
Gobi /góbi/7/44
goggles /gágəlz/35/15; 40/28
good /gud/75/8a
goose /gus/60/25
gorilla /gərílə/57/14
gown /gáun/16/24
granddaughter /grǽn-dɔtər/71/12
grandson /grǽn-sən/71/12
grandstand /grǽnd-stænd/47/5
grape /grep/61/12
grapefruit /grép-frut/61/30
grass /græs/26/21
grasshopper /grǽshapər/59/12
grenade /grənéd/45/9
grill /grıl/38/27
groundcloth /gráund-klɔθ/35/2
group /grup/72/11
group of tourists /grúp-əv-tərısts/72/11
guard /gard/16/13
guided missile /gáıdıd-mísəl/45/4
guitar /gıtár/49/26
gulf /gəlf/6
Gulf of Alaska /gálf-əv-əlǽskə/6/15
Gulf of Guinea /gálf-əv-gíni/6/19
Gulf of Mexico /gálf-əv-méksıko/6/17
gull /gəl/60/21
gun /gən/16/2; 45/6
gutter /gátər/14/9; 26/16

hacksaw /hǽk-sɔ/25/18
hair /hær/8/9
hairbrush /hǽr-brəš/32/21
hairdresser /hǽr-drɛsər/54/1
hair dryer /hǽr-draıər/31/14
half /hæf/69/12
half moon /hǽf-mún/4/12
hall /hɔl/28
hammer /hǽmər/25/14
hamper /hǽmpər/33/28
hand /hænd/8/27
hand brake /hǽnd-brek/38/19
handcuffs /hǽn-kəfs/16/8
hand drill /hǽn-drıl/25/3
hand grenade /hǽn-grəned/45/9
handkerchief /hǽŋkərčıf/13/9
handle /hǽndəl/25/16
handlebars /hǽndəl-barz/40/6
hangar /hǽŋər/44/21
happy /hǽpi/74/11a
hard /hard/74/13b
hard liquor /hárd-líkər/51/17
hat /hæt/11/13
hatchet /hǽčıt/25/7
hawk /hɔk/60/6
hay /he/36/2
hayloft /hé-lɔft/36/1
head /hɛd/8/10; 25/15
headboard /héd-bɔrd/32/2
headlight /héd-laıt/38/29; 40/5
heart /hart/9/23
heavy /hévi/75/12b
hedge /hɛj/27/17; 34/14
hedgehog /hɛj-hɔg/56/26
heel /hil/9/38; 11/11
height /haıt/69/9
helicopter /hélıkaptər/44/15
helmet /hɛlmıt/47/2
hem /hɛm/53/4
hen /hɛn/36/33
herd /hərd/72/10
herd of cattle /hərd-əv-kætəl/72/10
hero /héran/60/15
herring /hérıŋ/58/6
hibiscus /haıbískəs/62/24
high /haı/74/14a
hill /hıl/34/10
Himalayas /hıməléaz/7/40
hinge /hınj/28/5
hip /hıp/8/18
hip-bone /híp-bon/8/7
hippopotamus /hıpəpátəməs/57/20

hit /hɪt/66/5
hobby /hábi/52
hod /hɑd/23/18
hold /hold/42/8; 66/20
hole puncher /hól-pənčər/21/6
hollow /hálo/75/14b
homeplate /hom-plét/48/4
hood /hud/38/26
hoof /huf/36/27
hook /huk/28/10; 48/21
hook and eye /húk-ən-aí/53/23
horizon /həráɪzən/42/1
horn /hɔrn/49/14; 56/9; 57/26
horse /hɔrs/36/25; 46/2; 56/1
horse-racing /hɔ́rs-resɪŋ/46
hose /hoz/17/3
hospital bed /háspɪtəl-bed/17/19
hospital ward /haspɪtəl-wɔrd/17
hot /hat/74/15a
hot dog /hát-dɔg/20/12
hotel /hotél/35/7
hot water faucet /hát-wɔ́tər-fɔsɪt/33/2
hour hand /áuər-hænd/70/2
house /háus/26
household /háus-hold/31
hubcap /háb-kæp/38/30
Hudson Bay /hádsən-bé/6/16
hug /həg/66/6
human /hyúmən/8
hummingbird /hámɪŋ-bərd/60/27
hump /həmp/56/7
husband /házbənd/71/1
hydrant /háɪdrənt/17/4
hypoteneuse /haɪpátənus/68/12

icecream /áɪs-krím/35/17
ice skater /áɪs-sketər/47/30
ice skates /áɪs-skets/47/31
icicle /áɪsɪkəl/27/8
ignition /ɪgníšən/38/14
illustration /ɪləstréšən/52/20
in /ɪn/76/10
in box /ín-baks/21/12
Indian /índiən/6/13
Indus /índəs/7/51
in front of /ɪn-fránt-əv/76/7
insect /ínsekt/59
inside /ɪnsáɪd/76/10
inside lane /ínsaɪd-lén/39/6
insides /ɪnsáɪdz/9
instep /ínstep/9/39
intersection /íntərsekšən/14/15
intestines /ɪntéstɪnz/9/27
into /ɪn-tu/76/9
iris /áɪrɪs/9/20
iron /áɪərn/31/11; 66/18
ironing board /áɪərnɪŋ-bɔrd/31/3
irrigation canal /ɪrɪgéšən-kənæl/36/17
island /áɪlənd/5/12

jack of clubs /jǽk-əv-kləbz/52/11
jacket /jǽkɪt/10/7, 19; 11/27; 13/7; 29/22; 52/17
jail /jel/16
jar /jar/67/6
jaw /jɔ/9/9
jeans /jinz/10/14; 13/14
jeep /jip/45/5
jellyfish /jéli-fɪš/58/11
jet engine /jét-énjɪn/44/12
jewelry box /júəlri-baks/32/24
jigger /jígər/51/34
jockey /jáki/46/1
jodhpurs /jádpərz/46/8
judge /jəj/16/22
judo /júdo/46
judo suit /júdo sut/46/23
jump /jəmp/64/21
jury /jári/16/17

Kalahari /kaləhári/7/42
kangaroo /kæŋgərú/57/6
keel /kil/43/5
kettle /kétəl/30/17
key /ki/49/16
kick /kɪk/64/22
kidney /kídni/9/26
king /kɪŋ/52/8

kingfisher /kíŋfɪšər/60/30
king of hearts /kíŋ-əv-hárts/52/13
kiss /kɪs/66/7
kitchen /kíčɪn/30
kite /káɪt/35/30
kitten /kítən/56/16
knee /ni/8/34
kneecap /ní-kæp/8/8
kneesock /ní-sak/13/12
kneel /nil/64/23
knife /náɪf/30/31
knight /náɪt/52/5
knitting /nítɪŋ/53/21
knitting needle /nítɪŋ-nidəl/53/18

lab /læb/19
label /lébəl/22/21
laboratory /lǽbrətori/19
lace /les/53/9
ladder /lǽdər/17/8; 23/5
lake /lek/5/13; 34/5
lamb /læm/36/30
lamp /læmp/17/18; 29/26
lamp shade /lǽmp-šed/29/27
lapel /ləpél/11/15
large /larj/74/1a
last /læst/75/10b
launch pad /lɔ́nč-pæd/4/17
launching pad /lɔ́nčɪŋ-pæd/4/17
laundry /lɔ́ndri/27/29
law /lɔ/16
lawn /lɔn/27/19
leaf /lif/63/15
leap /lip/64/21
leaves /livz/27/15
left end /léft-énd/47/18
left fielder /léft-fíldər/48/15
left guard /left-gárd/47/16
left halfback /left-hǽlf-bæk/47/11
left lane /læft-lén/39/5
left tackle /læft-tǽkəl/47/17
leg /leg/8/32
leisure /lížər/50
lemon /lémən/61/14
length /leŋkθ/69/11
lens /lenz/19/10; 52/26
leopard /lépərd/57/18
lettuce /létəs/62/12
level /lévəl/23/19
librarian /laɪbrǽriən/50/22
library /láɪbræri/50
license plate /láɪsəns-plet/38/28
lick /lɪk/64/25
lie /láɪ/65/3
light /láɪt/17/18; 28/16; 47/7; 75/11a, 12a
light aircraft /láɪt-ǽrkræft/44/17
light-bulb /láɪt-bəlb/31/13
lighter /láɪtər/51/14
lightning /láɪtnɪŋ/27/1
light-switch /láɪt-swɪč/28/17
line /láɪn/48/20; 68/
line of latitude /láɪn-əv-lætɪtud/5/15
line of longitude /láɪn-əv-lɔnjɪtud/5/14
linesman /láɪnzmən/47/21
line-up /láɪn-əp/47
lion /láɪən/57/16
lip /lɪp/9/13
lipstick /lípstɪk/12/18
listen /lísən/65/1
litchi /líči/61/26
little /lítəl/74/16
liver /lívər/9/26
living-room /lívɪŋ-rum/29
lizard /lízərd/59/9
llama /lámə/56/5
loaf /lof/73/6
loafer /lófər/10/10
loaf of bread /lof-əv-bréd/73/6
lobster /lábstər/58/12
lock /lak/28/3
locust /lókəst/59/10
log /lɔg/63/18
long /lɔŋ/74/16a
longshoreman /lɔ́ŋ-šórmən/54/6
loose /lus/75/16a
loose-leaf notebook /lús-lif-not-buk/18/18
loose-leaf paper /lús-lif-pépər/18/17
loud /láud/75/13a

loudspeaker /láud-spikər/49/28
low /lo/74/14b
luggage /lágɪj/44/4
luggage rack /lágɪj-ræk/41/9
lump /ləmp/73/7
lump of sugar /ləmp-əv-šugər/73/7
lung /ləŋ/9/24

machine gun /məšín-gən/45/15
magazine /mǽgəzin/29/15
magazine rack /mǽgəzin-ræk/29/14
magnet /mǽgnət/19/19
magnifying-glass /mǽgnɪfaɪɪŋ-glæs/16/10
mailbag /mél-bæg/22/6
mailbox /mél-baks/14/1; 22/4
mailman /mél-mæn/22/5
mail slot /mél-slat/28/2
mallet /mǽlət/25/1
mane /men/36/26; 57/17
mango /mǽŋgo/61/15
mantel /mǽntəl/29/5
mantis /mǽntɪs/59/15
map /mæp/5; 18/19
mascara /mæskǽrə/12/13
mask /mæsk/35/15
mast /mæst/43/3
mat /mæt/28/6
match /mǽč/51/6
match book /mǽč-baks/51/5
material /mətíriəl/53/13
mattress /mǽtrɪs/32/8
meadow /médo/34/11
measurement /méžərmənt/69
meat /mit/20/13
mechanic /məkǽnɪk/54/5
medical /médɪkəl/17
medicine chest /médɪsɪn-čest/33/11
Mediterranean Sea /meditəréniən-sí/6/22
Mekong /mékɔŋ/7/53
men /men/10
menu /ményu/51/24
meter /mítər/19/4; 40/23
microphone /maɪkrəfon/49/25
microscope /maɪkrəskop/19/9
milk /mɪlk/20/10
miner /máɪnər/54/7
minus /máɪnəs/69/17
minute hand /mínɪt-hænd/70/1
mirror /mírər/32/13; 40/3
Mississippi /mɪsɪsípi/7/45
mitt /mɪt/48/7
money order /máni-ɔrdər/22/18
monkey /máŋki/57/12
monkey wrench /máŋki-renč/24/9
Moon /mun/4/6
mop /map/31/5
mortar /mɔ́rtər/19/21
mosquito /məskíto/59/20
moth /mɔθ/59/26
mother /máðər/71/4
mother-in-law /máðər-ɪn-lɔ/71/6
motorboat /mótər-bot/35/34; 43/11
motorcycle /mótər-saɪkəl/14/16; 39/20
mountain /máuntən/34/2
mountain peak /máuntan pik/34/3
mountain range /mauntən-renj/7
mouse /máus/56/18
mouth /máuθ/9/4
mouthpiece /máuθ-pis/49/23
movie theater /múvi-θitər/50/17
movies /múviz/50
mudguard /mád-gard/40/10
mug /məg/51/3
multiply by /máltɪplaɪ baɪ/69/16
muscle /másəl/9/31
mushroom /mášrum/62/14
music /myúzɪk/49; 49/12
musician /myuzíšən/49/3
mustache /məstǽš/9/10

nail /nel/8/31; 25/11
nail-file /nél-faɪl/12/11
nail-brush /nél-brəš/33/20
nail polish /nél-palɪš/12/14
napkin /nǽpkɪn/30/28; 51/32
napkin holder /nǽpkɪn-holdər/30/29
narrow /nǽro/75/1a
national defense /nǽšənəl-dífens/45

navigator /nǽvɪgetər/**45**/26
Navy /névi/**45**
near /nɪr/**76**/15
neat /nit/**75**/7a
neck /nɛk/**8**/11
necklace /nɛkləs/**12**/10
needle /nídəl/**5**/16; **53**/6; **63**/22
negative /négatɪv/**52**/23
nephew /néfyu/**71**/11
nest /nɛst/**60**/29
new /nu/**75**/3a
new moon /nú-mún/**4**/11
newspaper /núz-pepər/**29**/12
next to /nékst-tu/**76**/14
niece /nis/**71**/11
Niger /nájər/**7**/49
nightgown /náɪt-gaun/**12**/5
night table /náɪt-tebəl/**32**/9
nightstick /náɪt-stɪk/**16**/7
Nile /naɪl/**7**/48
nipple /nípəl/**32**/34
north /nɔrɵ/**5**/16
North America /nɔrɵ-əmérɪkə/**6**/1
North Atlantic /nɔrɵ-ətlǽntɪk/**6**/11
northeast /nɔ́rɵ-íst/**5**/16
North Pacific /nɔrɵ-pəsífɪk/**6**/9
North Pole /nɔ́rɵ-pól/**5**/1
North Sea /nɔ́rɵ-sí/**6**/20
northwest /nɔ́rɵ-wést/**5**/16
nose /noz/**9**/2
nosecone /nóz-kon/**4**/15
notebook /nót-bʊk/**18**/18
noun /náun/**72**; 73
nozzle /názəl/**17**/9
nurse /nərs/**17**/25; **55**/10
nut /nət/**25**/13
nutmeat /nát-mit/**61**/28

oar /ɔr/**43**/7
oarlock /ɔ́r-lak/**43**/8
oak tree /ók-tri/**63**/10
objects /ábjɛkts/31
oblong /áblɔŋ/**68**
obtuse angle /əbtús-ǽŋgəl/**68**/10
occupation /akyupéšən/**54–55**
ocean /óšən/**6**
ocean liner /óšən-laɪnər/**43**/20
o'clock /əklák/**70**/5
octopus /áktəpəs/**58**/23
off /ɔf/**77**/6
office /ɔ́fɪs/**21**
office building /ɔ́fɪs-bɪldɪŋ/**15**/19
oil-rig /ɔ́ɪl-rɪg/**37**/11
oil truck /ɔ́ɪl-trək/**39**/19
old /old/**75**/2b, 3b
old moon /óld-mún/**4**/14
olive /álɪv/**63**/3
on /an/**76**/12, 13
onion /ónyən/**62**/13
onto /an-tu/**76**/13
open /ópən/**65**/2; **74**/4b
operator /ápəretər/**21**/16
optician /aptíšən/**55**/14
orange /ɔ́rənj/**61**/16
orbit /ɔ́rbɪt/**4**/9
orchard /ɔ́rčərd/**36**/12
orchestra /ɔ́rkəstrə/**49**; **50**/11
orchestra pit /ɔ́rkəstrəpɪt/**50**/12
orchid /ɔ́rkɪd/**62**/21
ostrich /ástrɪč/**60**/1
out of /áut-əv/**76**/11
outboard motor /áutbɔrd-mótər/**43**/12
outlet /áut-lɛt/**31**/16
outside /autsáɪd/**76**/1
outside-lane /áutsaɪd-lén/**39**/5
outside wall /autsaɪd-wɔ́l/**26**/3
oval /ovál/**68**
oven /óvən/**30**/2
overcoat /óvər-kot/**11**/14
overpass /óvər-pæs/**39**/2
owl /áʊl/**60**/7
oyster /ɔ́ɪstər/**58**/16

page /peǰ/**52**/19
pail /pel/**31**/19
paint /pent/**65**/4
paintbrush /pént-brəš/**24**/14
paint can /pént-kæn/**24**/17
paint pan /pént-pæn/**24**/16
paint roller /pént-rolər/**24**/15
pajamas /pəjáməz/**10**/2
palm /pam/**8**/28; **63**/19
pan /pæn/**19**/2; **24**/16; **30**/13
panties /pǽntiz/**12**/3
pants /pǽnts/**11**/17
pantsuit /pǽnt-sut/**13**/2
pantyhose /pǽnti-hoz/**12**/4
papaya /pəpáɪə/**61**/25
paper bag /pepər-bǽg/**67**/2
paper clip /pépər-klɪp/**21**/9
paper cup /pepər-kə́p/**67**/8
parachute /pǽrəšut/**45**/25
parallel lines /pǽrəlel-láɪnz/**68**/5
park /park/**14**/11
parking lot /párkɪŋ-lat/**15**/29
parking meter /párkɪŋ-mitər/**15**/23
parrakeet /pǽrəkit/**60**/26
parrot /pǽrət/**60**/20
pass /pæs/**66**/13
passenger /pǽsɪnjər/**40**/26; **41**/19; **44**/6
passport /pǽs-pɔrt/**44**/3
path /pæɵ/**27**/18; **34**/17
patient /péšənt/**17**/20
patio /pǽtio/**26**/5
pattern /pǽtərn/**53**/20
paw /pɔ/**56**/17
pawn /pɔn/**52**/3
pea /pi/**62**/3
peach /pič/**61**/19
peacock /pí-kak/**60**/11
peak /pik/**34**/3
peanut /pí-nət/**61**/11
pear /per/**61**/22
pebble /pɛbəl/**35**/28
pedal /pédəl/**40**/17, **49**/17
peel /pil/**61**/6, 18
pelvis /pélvɪs/**8**/7
pen /pɛn/**18**/9; **36**/5
pencil /pénsəl/**18**/8
pencil holder /pénsəl-holdər/**21**/27
penguin /péngwɪn/**60**/13
pepper mill /pépər-mɪl/**51**/29
pepper shaker /pépər-šekər/**30**/40; **51**/30
per cent /pər-sént/**69**/20
perfume /pərfyum/**12**/15
periscope /pérɪskop/**45**/20
perpendicular line /pərpɪndíkyulər laɪn/**68**/4
Persian Gulf /pə́ržən-gə́lf/**6**/26
pestle /péstəl/**19**/20
petal /pétəl/**62**/20
phase /féz/**4**
pheasant /fézənt/**60**/14
photo /fóto/**52**/22
photocopier /fóto-kapiər/**21**/14
photograph /fótəgræf/**52**/22
photographer /fətágrəfər/**55**/4
photography /fətágrəfi/**52**
piano /piǽno/**49**/15
pick /pɪk/**66**/8
pick(ax) /pík-æks/**23**/12
piece /pis/**73**/8
piece of cake /pis-əv-kek/**73**/8
pier /pɪr/**42**/2
pig /pɪg/**56**/3
pigeon /píǰən/**60**/31
pile /páɪl/**72**/9, 12
pile of blankets /páɪl-əv-blǽŋkits/**72**/12
pile of stones /páɪl-əv-stónz/**72**/9
pillow /pílo/**32**/3
pillowcase /pílo-kes/**32**/4
pilot /páɪlət/**44**/5; **45**/27
pin /pɪn/**53**/12
pincer /pínsərz/**58**/18
pineapple /páɪnæpəl/**61**/24
pinecone /páɪn-kon/**63**/21
pine needles /páɪn-nidəlz/**63**/22
ping-pong /píŋ-pɔŋ/**46**
pip /pɪp/**61**/20
pipeline /páɪp-laɪn/**37**/12
pipette /paɪpét/**19**/18
pistol /pístəl/**45**/10
pit /pɪt/**50**/12; **61**/8; **20**

pitcher /pɪ́čər/**48**/8
pitchfork /pɪ́č-fɔrk/**27**/25
placemat /plés-mæt/**30**/30
plane /plen/**25**/2; **44**/9
planet /plǽnɪt/**4**/4
plant /plænt/**61–63**
plastic garden bag /plǽstɪk-gárdən-bæg/**67**/3
plastic wrap /plǽstɪk-ræp/**67**/10
plate /plet/**30**/34; **72**/13
plate of sandwiches /plet-əv-sǽndwɪčɪz/**72**/13
plateau /plætó/**34**/1
platform /plǽtfɔrm/**41**/20
platform number /plǽfɔrm-nəmbər/**41**/21
player /pléər/**49**/3
pleat /plit/**53**/11
pliers /pláɪərz/**25**/19
plow /pláu/**36**/19
plug /pləg/**31**/15
plum /pləm/**61**/23
plus /pləs/**69**/15
pneumatic drill /numǽtik-dríl/**23**/23
pocket /pákət/**11**/16
pocketknife /pákət-naɪf/**24**/5
pod /pad/**62**/4
pointer /pɔ́ɪntər/**19**/6
pole /pol/**47**/27
Pole /pol/**5**/A.1.7
police car /pəlís-kar/**16**/5
police dog /pəlís-dɔg/**16**/6
policeman /pəlísmən/**16**/1; **55**/13
police station /pəlís-stešən/**16**/4
pond /pand/**34**/19; **36**/9
pop group /páp-grup/**49**
porter /pɔ́rtər/**54**/14
postcard /póst-kard/**22**/14
postmark /póst-mark/**22**/8
post office /póst-ɔfɪs/**22**
postal clerk /póstəl-klərk/**22**/1
pot /pat/**30**/12
potato /pətéto/**20**/27; **62**/6
pouch /páuč/**57**/7
power /páuər/**37**
powerhouse /páuər-haus/**37**/3
power saw /páuər-sɔ/**24**/11
power station /páuər-stešən/**37**/6
preposition /prepəzíšən/**76–77**
pretty /príti/**75**/9a
prisoner /prízənər/**16**/14
profession /prəféšən/**54**; **55**
projectionist /prəjékšənɪst/**50**/16
projection room /prəjékšən-rum/**50**/14
projector /prəjéktər/**50**/15; **52**/29
propeller /prəpélər/**44**/18
prosecuting attorney /prásɪkyutɪŋ-ətártni/**16**/23
protractor /prótræktər/**18**/12
pull /pʊl/**65**/5
pump /pəmp/**40**/16
pupil /pyúpəl/**9**/19
puppy /pápi/**56**/19
purse /pərs/**13**/4
push /pʊš/**65**/6
put /pʊt/**66**/15
pylon /páɪlan/**37**/5
pyramid /pírəmɪd/**68**/22

quantity /kwántɪti/**72**
quarter /kwɔ́rtər/**69**/14
quarterback /kwɔ́rtə-bæk/**47**/8
queen /kwin/**52**/7
queen of diamonds /kwín-əv-dáɪəməndz/**52**/12

rabbit /rǽbɪt/**56**/20
racehorse /rés-hɔrs/**46**/2
racing /résɪŋ/**46**
rack /ræk/**28**/9
racket /rǽkɪt/**46**/19; **48**/27
radiator /rédietər/**38**/33
radio /redio/**29**/24
radius /rédiəs/**68**/17
rafter /rǽftər/**23**/3
railroad switch /rélrod-swɪč/**41**/26
railroad ties /rélrod-taɪz/**41**/25
railroad track /rélrod-træk/**41**/24
rain /ren/**27**/3
raincoat /rén-kot/**11**/12
raindrop /rén-drap/**27**/4
rainhat /rén-hæt/**11**/30

rat /ræt/**56**/22
rattle /rǽtəl/**32**/30
razor /rézər/**33**/13
razor-blade /rézər-bled/**33**/14
read /rid/**65**/7
reading /rídiŋ/**52**
rear light /rír-láit/**40**/30
rearview mirror /rír-vyu-mírər/**38**/1
receipt /rɪsít/**20**/23
receiver /rɪsívər/**28**/19
receptionist /rɪsépšənɪst/**21**/25
record /rékərd/**29**/21
record jacket /rékərd-jækət/**29**/22
recreation /rɛkriešən/**46–52**
rectangle /réktæŋəl/**68**
red cap /réd-kæp/**54**/14
Red Sea /réd-sí/**6**/25
referee /rɛfəri/**46**/10; **47**/3
refinery /rɪfáɪnəri/**37**/13
reflector /rɪflɛ́ktər/**40**/20
refrigerator /rɪfríjərɛtər/**30**/5
reindeer /réndɪr/**56**/11
reins /renz/**46**/4
relationship /rɪlɛ́šənšɪp/**71**
reptile /réptaɪl/**59**
reservoir /rézəvwar/**37**/1
restaurant /réstərant/**51**
return address /rɪtárn-ǽdrɛs/**22**/12
revolver /rɪválvər/**45**/12
rhinoceros /raɪnásərəs/**57**/25
rib /rɪb/**8**/5
ribbon /ríbən/**53**/24
rice /ráɪs/**63**/7
ride /ráɪd/**65**/8
rifle /ráɪfəl/**45**/2
right angle /ráɪt-æŋgəl/**68**/14
right end /raɪt-énd/**47**/12
right fielder /ráɪt-fíldər/**48**/17
right guard /raɪt-gárd/**47**/9
right halfback /raɪt-hǽf-bæk/**47**/9
right lane /raɪt-lén/**39**/6
right tackle /raɪt-tǽkəl/**47**/13
rind /raɪnd/**61**/18
ring /rɪŋ/**12**/7; **46**/13
river /rívər/**7**; **34**/12
road /rod/**15**/31; **34**/18; **38–40**
robe /rob/**16**/24
rock /rak/**35**/29
rocket /rákət/**4**/16
Rockies /rákiz/**7**/36
rod /rad/**48**/19
roll /rol/**73**/12
roller /rólər/**12**/22; **24**/15
roll of film /ról-əv-fílm/**52**/24
roll of paper /ról-əv-pépər/**73**/12
roof /ruf/**26**/1
rook /ruk/**52**/14
rooster /rústər/**36**/34
root /rut/**63**/11
rope /rop/**46**/14
rose /roz/**62**/19
rostrum /rástrəm/**49**/13
rotor /rótər/**44**/16
rough /rəf/**75**/4b. 5a
row /rol/**72**/14
row of houses /ró-əv-háuzɪz/**72**/14
rowboat /ró-bot/**43**/6
rubber boot /rábər-bút/**10**/12
rubber tubing /rábər-túbiŋ/**19**/14
rudder /rádər/**43**/4
ruffle /rəfəl/**53**/14
rug /rəg/**28**/8; **32**/17
ruler /rúlər/**18**/10
run /rən/**65**/9
rung /rəŋ/**23**/6
runway /ránwe/**44**/19

sack /sæk/**20**/6; **67**/2
sad /sæd/**72**/11b
saddle /sǽdəl/**36**/28; **46**/3
saddlebag /sǽdəl-bæg/**40**/8. 34
safety belt /séfti-belt/**38**/24
safety pin /séfti-pɪn/**53**/10
Sahara /səhǽrə/**7**/41
sail /sel/**43**/2; **65**/10
sailboat /sél-bot/**43**/1
sailor /sélər/**55**/15

salesman /sélzmən/**55**/9
salmon /sǽmən/**58**/4
saltshaker /sɔ́lt-šekər/**30**/39; **51**/28
sand /sænd/**23**/15; **35**/22
sandal /sǽndəl/**13**/17
sandcastle /sǽnd-kæsəl/**35**/23
sandpaper /sǽnd-pepər/**24**/3
sandwich bag /sǽnwɪč-bæg/**67**/4
satellite /sǽtəlaɪt/**4**/18
saw /sɔ/**25**/17
saxophone /sǽksɪfon/**49**/22
scaffolding /skǽfəldɪŋ/**23**/7
scale /skel/**22**/2; **33**/24; **59**/7
scales /skelz/**19**/1; **58**/9
scarecrow /skɛ́r-kro/**36**/13
scarf /skarf/**11**/19
schedule /skéjəl/**41**/15
school /skul/**18**
science /sáɪəns/**19**
scissors /sízərz/**53**/26
scooter /skútər/**40**/29
scoreboard /skɔr-bórd/**47**/23
scorpion /skɔ́rpiən/**58**/27
scouring powder /skáurɪŋ-paudər/**31**/9
screen /skrin/**50**/18; **52**/27
screw /skru/**25**/9
screwdriver /skrú-draɪvər/**24**/7
scrub brush /skráb-brəš/**31**/10
sea /si/**6–7**; **35**
seagull /sí-gəl/**58**/12
Sea of Japan /sí-əv-jəpǽn/**7**/33
Sea of Okhotsk /sí-əv-okátsk/**7**/34
seal /sil/**57**/9
seam /sim/**53**/3
seashell /sí-šel/**35**/27
seaside /sí-saɪd/**35**
seat /sit/**38**/23; **40**/7, 30; **41**/8; **50**/20
seat-belt /sít-belt/**38**/24
seawall /sí-wɔl/**35**/10
seaweed /sí-wid/**35**/37
second hand /sékənd-hænd/**70**/3
second baseman /sɛkənd-bésmən/**48**/11
secretary /sékrətæri/**21**/22
section /sékšən/**61**/17; **68**/21
sedan /sɪdǽn/**38**/37
seed /sid/**62**/28
server /sávər/**48**/25
service /sárvɪs/**17**
service line /sárvɪs-laɪn/**48**/26
set /sɛt/**50**/4
sew /so/**65**/11
sewer /súər/**14**/10
sewing /sóɪŋ/**53**
sewing machine /sóɪŋ-məšin/**53**/1
shallow /šǽlo/**74**/6a
shape /šep/**68**
shark /šark/**58**/1
sharp /šarp/**74**/2b
shaving brush /šévɪŋ-brəš/**33**/16
shaving mug /šévɪŋ-məg/**33**/15
shed /šɛd/**26**/20; **27**/26
sheep /šip/**36**/29
sheet /šit/**32**/5
sheet music /šít-myuzɪk/**49**/12
shelf /šɛlf/**20**/15; **24**/18; **29**/17; **30**/16
shell /šɛl/**45**/7; **58**/14; **59**/5
shingle /šɪŋgəl/**23**/4
ship /šɪp/**42**/7
shirt /šərt/**11**/1; **13**/15
shoe /šu/**10**/11; **11**/8
shoelace /šú-les/**11**/9
shoot /šut/**65**/12
shopping bag /šápɪŋ-bæg/**67**/18
shopping basket /šápɪŋ-bæskɪt/**20**/7
shopping cart /šápɪŋ-kart/**20**/1
short /šɔrt/**74**/16b
shorts /šɔrts/**10**/5
shortstop /šɔ́rt-stap/**48**/12
shoulder /šóldər/**8**/13
shoulder bag /šóldər-bæg/**13**/4
shoulder-blade /šóldər-bled/**8**/3
shovel /šávəl/**23**/13; **35**/25
shower curtain. /šáuər-kərtən/**33**/31
shower head /šáuər-hed/**33**/4
shut /šət/**65**/13; **74**/4a
shutter /šátər/**26**/12
side /sáɪd/**68**/13; **69**/5
sidewalk /sáɪd-wɔk/**15**/26
siding /sáɪdɪŋ/**41**/30

signal /sígnəl/**41**/27
signal box /sígnəl-baks/**41**/23
signalman /sígnəlmən/**41**/22
sill /sɪl/**26**/11
sing /sɪŋ/**65**/14
singer /síŋər/**49**/24
sink /sɪŋk/**30**/7; **33**/12
sister /sístər/**71**/5
sister-in-law /sístər-in-lɔ/**71**/8
sit /sɪt/**65**/15
site /sáɪt/**23**
sixteenth /sɪkstínθ/**70**/11
skate /sket/**47**/31
skater /sketər/**47**/30
skeleton /skɛ́lətən/**8**
ski /ski/**47**/26
skier /skíər/**47**/25
skillet /skílɪt/**30**/14
skin /skɪn/**61**/3
ski-pole /skí-pol/**47**/27
skirt /skərt/**13**/8
skull /skəl/**8**/1
sky /skáɪ/**27**/10
slacks /slæks/**10**/8; **11**/29
sleep /slip/**66**/19
sleeper /slípər/**32**/7
sleeping bag /slípɪŋ-bæg/**35**/3
sleeve /sliv/**11**/7
slide /sláɪd/**19**/11; **49**/21; **52**/30
slide projector /sláɪd-prəjɛktər/**52**/29
slide rule /sláɪd-rul/**18**/16
sling /slɪŋ/**17**/23
slip /slɪp/**12**/2
slipper /slípər/**10**/3; **12**/6
sloppy /slápi/**75**/7b
slow /slo/**74**/9b
slug /sləg/**58**/19
small /smɔl/**74**/1b
smile /smaɪl/**65**/16
smoke /smok/**17**/13
smokestack /smók-stæk/**37**/7; **42**/9; **43**/21
smooth /smuð/**75**/5b
snail /snel/**58**/13
snake /snek/**59**/6
snap /snæp/**53**/27
sneaker /sníkər/**10**/13
snorkel /snɔ́rkəl/**35**/16
snout /snáut/**56**/4; **58**/8
snow /sno/**27**/5
snowball /snó-bɔl/**27**/6
snowman /snó-mæn/**27**/7
soap /sop/**33**/27
soap powder /sóp-paudər/**20**/28; **31**/18
sock /sak/**10**/6; **13**/12
socket /sákɪt/**31**/16
sofa /sófə/**29**/9
soft /sɔft/**74**/13a; **75**/13b
softdrink /sɔ́ft-dríŋk/**51**/13
soldier /sóljər/**45**/1; **55**/12
sole /sol/**9**/40; **11**/10
solid /sálɪd/**75**/14a
solid figures /sálɪd-fígyərz/**68**
son /sən/**71**/3
son-in-law /sán-ɪn-lɔ/**71**/7
south /sauθ/**5**/16
South America /sauθ-əmérɪkə/**6**/2
South Atlantic /sauθ-ətlǽntɪk/**6**/12
South China Sea /sáuθ-čáɪnə-sí/**7**/31
southeast /sáuθ-íst/**5**/16
Southern /sáðərn/**6**/14
South Pacific /sauθ-pəsífɪk/**6**/10
South Pole /sáuθ-pól/**5**/7
southwest /sáuθ-wést/**5**/16
space /spes/**4**
space-capsule /spés-kæpsəl/**4**/19
spacesuit /spés-sut/**4**/21
space-travel /spés-trævəl/**4**
spark plug /spárk-pləg/**38**/35
sparrow /spǽro/**60**/28
speaker /spíkər/**29**/20; **49**/28
speedometer /spidámətər/**38**/16
spider /spáɪdər/**58**/25
spider web /spáɪdər-web/**58**/26
spin /spɪn/**66**/16
spine /spáɪn/**8**/6; **52**/18
spiral /spáɪrəl/**68**/1
spoke /spok/**40**/12
sponge /spənj/**33**/26

spool of thread /spul/(/əv θréd/) **53**/8; **73**/9
spoon /spun/**30**/32
port /spɔrt/**46–48**
sportcoat /spɔ́rt-kot/**10**/7; **11**/27
sports car /spɔ́rts-kar/**39**/18
sports coupe /spɔ́rts-kup/**38**/39
spotlight /spát-laɪt/**50**/7
sprocket /sprákɪt/**40**/19
square /skwær/**68**
squash /skwaš/**62**/7
squirrel /skwɔ́rəl/**56**/19
stadium /stédiəm/**47**
stage /steǰ/**50**/1
stair /stɛr/**28**/11
staircase /stɛ́rkes/**28**/12
stalk /stɔk/**61**/2; **62**/2
stamp /stæmp/**22**/9
stand /stænd/**47**/5; **52**/28; **65**/17
stapler /stéplər/**21**/7
star /star/**4**/5
starter /stártər/**40**/36
station /stéšən/**41**/13
station wagon /stešən-wægən/**38**/40
stein /staɪn/**51**/3
steering wheel /stíriŋ-hwil/**38**/17
stem /stɛm/**62**/23
stenographer /stənɔ́grəfər/**16**/25
steno pad /sténo-pæ/**21**/23
stern /stərn/**43**/14
stethoscope /stéθəskop/**17**/22
steward /stúərd/**44**/8
stewardess /stúərdəs/**44**/7
stick /stɪk/**46**/18
stir /stər/**65**/18
stirrup /stárəp/**46**/7
stitch /stɪč/**53**/17
stomach /stómək/**8**/17
stone /ston/**61**/8, 20
stool /stul/**19**/8; **32**/12; **49**/18; **51**/21
storage tank /stɔ́rɪǰ-tæŋk/**37**/14
store /stɔr/**15**/20
storm cloud /stɔ́rm-klaud/**27**/2
stove /stov/**30**/1
straight /stret/**74**/5b
straight line /strét-láɪn/**68**/2
straight pin /strét-pɪn/**53**/12
straw /strɔ/**51**/12
strawberry /strɔ́bɛri/**61**/21
stream /strim/**34**/7
street /strit/**15**/31
street light /strít-laɪt/**15**/22
street sign /strít-saɪn/**14**/7
string /strɪŋ/**22**/20; **49**/5; **72**/8
string of beads /stríŋ-əv-bídz/**72**/8
strong /strɔŋ/**75**/6a
student /stúdənt/**18**/5
stuffed animal /stə́ft-ænɪməl/**32**/29
submarine /sə́bmərin/**45**/19
subway station /sə́bwe-stešən/**14**/3
sugar cane /šúgər-ken/**63**/9
sugar-bowl /šúgər-bol/**30**/38
suit /sut/**11**/6; **13**/5
suit jacket /sút-ǰækɪt/**13**/7
suitcase /sút-kes/**67**/19
sun /sən/**4**/8; **27**/9
sun-bather /sə́n-beðər/**35**/13
sunfish /sə́n-fɪš/**58**/15
sunflower /sə́n-flauər/**62**/27
supermarket /súpər-markɪt/**20**
surf /sərf/**35**/32
swallow /swálo/**60**/22
swan /swan/**60**/17
swarm /swɔrm/**72**/16
swarm of bees /swɔ́rm-əv-bíz/**72**/16
sweater /swétər/**10**/9, 15; **13**/16
sweep /swip/**65**/19
swim /swɪm/**65**/20
swimmer /swímər/**35**/35
switch /swɪč/**28**/17; **31**/17; **41**/26
switchboard /swíč-bɔrd/**21**/15
swordfish /sɔ́rd-fɪš/**58**/3

T-formation /tí-fɔrmešən/**47**/19
T-shirt /tí-šərt/**10**/4
table /tébəl/**30**/26; **46**/21
table-cloth /tébəl-klɔθ/**51**/31
table-tennis /tébəl-tɛnɪs/**46**
tail /tel/**44**/13; **56**/23; **57**/2; **58**/7
tail fin /tél-fɪn/**44**/13

taillight /tél-laɪt/**38**/4
tank /tæŋk/**45**/8
tanker /tǽŋkər/**43**/18
tap /tæp/**51**/20
tape /tep/**53**/2
tape measure /tép-mɛžər/**53**/25
Tasman Sea /tǽzmən-sí/**6**/30
taxi /tǽksi/**14**/4
taxicab /tǽksi-kæb/**14**/4; **40**/22
taxi driver /tǽksi-draɪvər/**40**/25
taxi stand /tǽksi-stænd/**40**/21
tea /ti/**63**/8
teacher /tíčər/**18**/1; **55**/11
tea kettle /tí-kɛtəl/**30**/17
team /tím/**72**/15
team of players /tím-əv-pléərz/**72**/15
tear /tɪr/**65**/21
telegram /téləgræm/**22**/17
telephone /téləfon/**21**/2; **28**/18
telephone book /téləfon-buk/**28**/22
telephone-booth /téləfon-buθ/**15**/28
television /téləvɪžən/**29**/29
temperature /tɛmpəčur/**70**
temple /tɛmpəl/**9**/7
tennis /ténɪs/**48**
tennis ball /ténɪs-bɔl/**48**/28
tennis court /ténɪs-kɔrt/**48**/23
tennis racket /ténɪs-rækɪt/**48**/27
tennis shoe /tɛnɪs-šu/**10**/13
tent /tɛnt/**35**/1
tentacle /téntəkəl/**58**/24
test tube /tést-tub/**19**/22
text /tɛkst/**52**/21
theater /θíétər/**50A**; **50**/8
thermometer /θərmámɪtər/**70**/12
thermos /θə́rməs/**67**/9
thick /θɪk/**75**/15a
thigh /θáɪ/**8**/33
thimble /θímbəl/**53**/5
thin /θɪn/**74**/10b; **75**/15b
third /θərd/**69**/13
third baseman /θərd-bésmən/**48**/13
thread /θrɛd/**25**/10; **53**/8
throat /θrot/**8**/12
through /θru/**76**/2
throw /θro/**66**/9
thruway /θrúwe/**39**/1
thumb /θəm/**8**/29
ticket /tíkɪt/**41**/1
ticket office /tíkɪt-ɔfɪs/**41**/14
tie /táɪ/**11**/4; **65**/23
ties /táɪz/**41**/25
tiger /táɪgər/**57**/19
tight /táɪt/**75**/16b
tile /táɪl/**33**/29
time /táɪm/**70**
tire /táɪr/**38**/8; **40**/11
to /tu/**77**/4
toaster /tóstər/**30**/18
toboggan /təbágən/**47**/29
tobogganist /təbágənɪst/**47**/28
toe /to/**9**/41
toilet /tɔ́ɪlɪt/**33**/8
toilet-paper /tɔ́ɪlɪt-pepər/**33**/10
tomato /təméto/**62**/15
tongue /təŋ/**9**/14; **59**/8
tool /tul/**26**
tool shed /túl-šed/**26**/20
tooth /tuθ/**9**/12
toothbrush /túθ-brəš/**33**/17
toothpaste /túθ-pest/**33**/21
top /tap/**69**/1
torpedo /tɔrpído/**45**/17
tortoise /tɔ́rtəs/**59**/2
touch /təč/**65**/22
toward /tɔrd/**77**/10
towel /táuəl/**33**/22; **35**/14
towel rack /táuəl-ræk/**33**/23
toy /tɔɪ/**32**/19
toybox /tɔ́ɪ-baks/**32**/18
track /træk/**41**/24
tractor /træktər/**36**/18
traffic-light /trǽfik-laɪt/**14**/6
trailer /trélər/**39**/13, 21
trailer truck /trélər-trək/**39**/11
train /tren/**41**/1
train station /trén-stešən/**41**/13
transporter /trǽnzpɔrtər/**39**/12
trash can /træš-kæn/**15**/27; **67**/12

travel /trǽvəl/**38–44**
trawler /trɔlər/**43**/17
tree /tri/**27**/11; **34**/15
trenchcoat /trénč-kot/**11**/12
triangle /tráɪæŋgəl/**68**
trigger /trígər/**45**/13
tripod /tráɪpad/**19**/13
trombone /trambón/**49**/20
Tropic of Cancer /trápɪk-əv-kǽnsər/**5**/3
Tropic of Capricorn /trápɪk-əv-kǽprɪkɔrn/**5**/5
trousers /trauzərz/**11**/17
trowel /tráuəl/**23**/17
truck /trək/**14**/14; **39**/14
truck driver /trə́k-draɪvər/**54**/12
trumpet /trómpət/**49**/19
trunk /trəŋk/**27**/12; **38**/2; **57**/22; **63**/12; **67**/16
trunks /trəŋks/**35**/20
tub /təb/**33**/1
tube /tub/**73**/13
tube of toothpaste /túb-əv-túθ-pest/**73**/13
tulip /túlɪp/**62**/22
turkey /tə́rki/**60**/16
turn /tərn/**66**/10
turn signal /tə́rn-sɪgnəl/**38**/5
turntable /tə́rn-tebəl/**29**/19
turtle /tə́rtəl/**59**/4
turtleneck sweater /tə́rtəl nɛk swétər/**13**/1
tusk /təsk/**57**/23
TV /tí-ví/**29**/28
twig /twɪg/**27**/14; **63**/14
type /táɪp/**66**/21
typewriter /táɪp-raɪtər/**21**/21
typist /táɪpɪst/**54**/9

ugly /ə́gli/**75**/9b
umbrella /əmbrélə/**11**/24
umpire /ə́mpaɪər/**48**/3
uncle /ə́ŋkəl/**71**/10
under /ə́ndər/**76**/17
underneath /əndərníθ/**76**/17
underpass /ə́ndər-pæs/**39**/3
undershirt /ə́ndər-šərt/**10**/4
(under)shorts /ə́ndər-šɔrts/**10**/5
uniform /yúnɪfɔrm/**16**/3
universe /yúnɪvərs/**4**
up /əp/**76**/5
upper arm /ə́pər-árm/**8**/22
upstairs /əpstérz/**28**/14
Urals /yúrəlz/**7**/39
usher /ə́šər/**50**/19

vacuum cleaner /vǽkyəm-klinər/**31**/1
valley /vǽli/**34**/6
valve /vælv/**40**/13; **49**/2
van /væn/**14**/13; **39**/22
vegetables /véǰtəbəlz/**20**/18; **62**
vein /ven/**9**/29
verb /vərb/**64–66**
vest /vɛst/**11**/5
village /vílɪǰ/**34**/16
vine /váɪn/**61**/13
viola /vióla/**49**/7
violin /vaɪəlín/**49**/4
vise /vaɪs/**24**/8
vulture /vólčər/**60**/10

waist /west/**8**/16
waiter /wétər/**51**/22
waiting room /wétɪŋ-rum/**41**/18
waitress /wétrəs/**54**/11
walk /wɔk/**65**/24
wall /wɔl/**26**/3; **29**/2
wallet /wálɪt/**67**/21
walnut /wɔ́lnət/**61**/27
warehouse /wǽr-haus/**42**/3
warship /wɔr-šɪp/**45**/16
wash /wɔš/**65**/25
wash cloth /wɔ́š-klɔθ/**33**/19
washer /wɔ́šər/**25**/12
washing machine /wɔ́šɪŋ-məšín/**31**/4
wasp /wasp/**59**/22
wastepaper basket /wés-pepər-bæskɪt/**21**/13
watch /wač/**11**/21
watchband /wáč-bænd/**11**/22
water /wɔ́tər/**35**/31; **42–43**
waterfall /wɔ́tər-fɔl/**34**/4
watering-can /wɔ́tərɪŋ-kæn/**27**/23

waterlily /wótərlɪli/**62**/26
wave /wev/**35**/33; **66**/1
wavy line /wévi-láɪn/**68**/7
weak /wik/**75**/6b
weather /wéðər/**27**
web /wɛb/**58**/26
webbed foot /wɛ́bd-fút/**60**/9
weep /wip/**64**/7
weight /we/**19**/3
west /wɛst/**5**/16
wet /wɛt/**74**/7a
whale /hwel/**57**/1
wharf /wɔrf/**42**/5
wheat /hwit/**36**/14; **63**/2
wheel /hwil/**40**/9
wheelbarrow /hwíl-bæro/**23**/24; **27**/27
whisker /hwískər/**56**/21
whistle /hwísəl/**41**/12
wide /wáɪd/**75**/1b
width /wɪdθ/**69**/8
wife /wáɪf/**71**/1
willow /wílo/**63**/24

wind /wind/**66**/3
windbreaker /wínd-brekər/**35**/18
windlass /wídləs/**42**/16
window /wíndo/**26**/8
window box /wíndo-baks/**26**/13
window frame /wíndo-frem/**26**/9
window pane /wíndo-pen/**26**/10
windowsill /wíndo-sɪl/**26**/11
windpipe /wínd-paɪp/**9**/22
windshield /wín-šild/**38**/10
windshield wiper /wín-šild-waɪpər/**38**/11
wine glass /wáɪn-glæs/**51**/27
wing /wɪŋ/**44**/11; **60**/23
wings /wɪŋz/**50**/5
winter sports /wíntər-spórts/**47**
witness /wítnɪs/**16**/19
witness stand /wítnɪs-stænd/**16**/18
wolf /wʊlf/**57**/11
women /wímɪn/**12–13**
wood /wʊd/**34**/8
wool /wʊl/**53**/19
workbench /wórk-bɛnč/**24**/1

workman /wórkmən/**23**/14
workshop /wórk-šap/**24**
world /wərld/**5–7**
worm /wərm/**58**/21
wrench /rɛnč/**24**/13
wrestler /réslər/**46**/22
wrestling /réslɪŋ/**46**
wrist /rɪst/**8**/25
write /ráɪt/**66**/2

x-ray /ɛ́ks-re/**17**/24

Yangtze /yǽŋ-tsí/**7**/55
yard /yard/**27**; **80**
Yellow River /yélo-rívər/**7**/54
young /yəŋ/**75**/2a

zebra /zíbrə/**57**/24
zigzag /zíg-zæg/**68**/6
zip code /zíp-kod/**22**/13
zipper /zípər/**53**/22

INDICE

a /**77**/4
abajo /**69**/2
abajo de /**76**/17
el abdomen /**59**/18
a abeja /**59**/21
el abeto /**63**/20
abierto /**74**/4b
el abogado defensor /**16**/21
abrazar /**66**/6
el abrelatas /**30**/21
el abrelatas eléctrico /**30**/19
el abrevadero /**36**/9
el abridor de botellas /**30**/23
el abrigo /**11**/14; **13**/11
abrir /**65**/2
el acantilado /**35**/6
la aceituna /**63**/3
el acelerador /**38**/18; **40**/32
la acequía /**36**/17
la acera /**14**/8; **15**/26
el acomodador /**50**/19
el actor /**50**/2
la actriz /**50**/3
el acumulador /**38**/32
el acusado /**16**/20
adjetivos /**74**; **75**
la aduana /**44**/1
el aduanero /**44**/2
el aereograma /**22**/7
el aerodeslizador /**42**/18
la aeromoza /**44**/7
el aeromozo /**44**/8
el aeropuerto /**44**
afilado /**74**/2b
Africa /**6**/4
afuera de /**76**/1, 11; **77**/6
la agalla /**58**/5
la agarradera del remo /**43**/8
agarrar /**66**/20
agitar /**66**/1
el agua /**35**/31
la aguamala /**59**/11
el águila /**60**/2
la aguja /**5**/16; **19**/6; **53**/6
la aguja de tejer /**53**/18
las agujas /**63**/22
ahogarse /**64**/16
el ajedrez /**52**, 1
ajustado /**75**/16b
el ajustador petrolero /**37**/11
el ala /**44**/11; **60**/23
el alacrán /**58**/27
las alas /**50**/5
el albañil /**23**/2
la alcarilla /**14**/10
la aldaba /**28**/2
la aldea /**34**/16
el alero /**26**/11
la aleta /**35**/21; **44**/13; **57**/2, 4, 10; **58**/2
el alféizar /**26**/11
el alfil /**52**/6
el alfiler /**53**/12
el alfiler de seguridad /**53**/10
la alfombra /**28**/8; **29**/3
la alfombrilla /**26**/18; **28**/6; **32**/17
la alfombrilla de baño /**33**/25
el alga /**35**/37
el algodón /**63**/6
el alhajero /**32**/24
el alicate /**25**/19
al lado de /**76**/14
el almacén /**42**/3
la almendra /**61**/28
la almohada /**32**/3
el almohadón /**29**/10
a lo largo de /**77**/9

los Alpes /**7**/38
alrededor de /**76**/6
la altiplanicie /**34**/1
alto /**74**/14a
la altura /**69**/9
la amapola /**62**/24
El Amarillo /**7**/54
El Amazonas /**7**/46
la ambulancia /**39**/15; **47**/24
la ametralladora /**45**/15
el amplificador /**29**/18; **49**/27
la ananá /**61**/24
el anaquel /**29**/14
ancho /**75**/1b
el ancho /**69**/8
el ancla /**42**/11
el andamio /**23**/7
la andanada /**47**/5
el andén /**41**/20
los Andes /**7**/37
angosto /**75**/1a
la anguila /**59**/10
el ángulo agudo /**68**/11
el ángulo derecho /**68**/14
el ángulo obtuso /**68**/10
el ángulo recto /**68**/14
el anillo /**12**/7
Los Animales /**56; 57; 58; 59; 60**
Antártica /**6**/7
el Antártico /**6**/14
el antebrazo /**8**/24
la antena /**26**/19; **38**/9; **59**/16, 24
los anteojos /**11**/23; **40**/28
los anteojos de protección /**40**/28
los anteojos submarinos /**35**/15
el antílope /**57**/5
el anzuelo /**48**/21
el apagador /**28**/17; **31**/17
el aparcadero /**41**/30
el ápice /**68**/8
aplaudir /**66**/17
apretado /**75**/16b
el arado /**36**/19
la arandela /**25**/12
la araña /**58**/25
el árbitro /**46**/10; **47**/3; **48**/6
el árbol /**27**/11; **34**/15
el árbol frutal /**36**/11
el arbusto /**27**/22
el arco /**49**/6; **68**/16
la ardilla /**56**/19
la arena /**23**/15; **35**/22
el arenque /**58**/6
el arete /**12**/9
el armario /**32**/14
arriba /**69**/1
arrodillarse /**64**/23
el arroyo /**34**/7
el arroz /**63**/7
la arteria /**9**/30
el Artico /**6**/8
Los Artículos del Hogar /**31**
el artista /**54**/8
el as de espadas /**52**/14
Asia /**6**/5
el asiento /**38**/23; **40**/7, 31; **41**/8
las asientos /**50**/20
áspero /**75**/5a
la aspiradora /**31**/1
la asta /**56**/12
el astronauta /**4**/20
atar /**65**/23
el Atlántico del Norte /**6**/11
el Atlántico del Sur /**6**/12
a través de /**76**/2
Australia /**6**/6
el autobús /**15**/24
el automóvil /**38**; **39**/16
el autoparlante /**49**/28

la autopista /**39**/1
la avenida /**35**/9
el avestruz /**60**/1
el avión de caza /**45**/21
el avión de combate /**45**/21
el avión de pasajeros /**44**/9
la avioneta /**44**/17
la avispa /**59**/22
la axila /**8**/20
la ayudante del dentista /**17**/14
la azafata /**44**/7
el azafate de pintura /**24**/16
el Azul /**7**/55

el babero /**32**/35
la babosa /**58**/19
la bahía /**5**/8
la Bahía de Hudson /**6**/16
Las Bahías /**6**
bailar /**64**/9
bajando por /**76**/4
bajo /**76**/3
la bala /**45**/11
la balanza /**19**/1; **22**/2; **33**/24
el balcón /**26**/4; **50**/10
el balconcesto /**46**
el balde /**31**/19; **35**/24
Balonpié /**47**
la ballena /**57**/1
el banco /**19**/7
el banco de trabajo /**24**/1
la bandada /**72**/6
la bandada de pájaros /**72**/6
la bandera /**41**/11
la banqueta /**14**/8; **15**/26
el banquito /**19**/8; **32**/12
la bañera /**33**/1
la bañista /**35**/35
baño /**33**
El Bar /**51**
La Baraja /**52**/b
la baranda /**28**/13
la barandilla /**28**/13
la barba /**9**/11
el barbero /**55**/6
la barbilla /**6**
la barcaza /**43**/16
el barco /**42**/7
la barra /**51**/15; **73**/3
la barra de jabón /**73**/3
barrer /**65**/19
la barrena /**25**/6
la barrera /**41**/17
el barril /**67**/13
la base /**68**/9
el basketball /**46**/C
la bastilla /**53**/4
el basurero /**30**/9
la bata /**10**/1; **12**/21
el bate /**48**/4
el bateador /**48**/5, 8
la batería /**38**/32
la batuta /**49**/11
el baúl /**38**/2; **67**/16
la bayoneta /**45**/3
el bebé /**32**
beber /**64**/13
la bebida /**51**/17
el becerro /**36**/22
El Beisbol /**48**
la bellota /**63**/16
el berbiquí /**25**/5
la berenjena /**62**/16
besar /**66**/7
el betabel /**62**/9
el biberón /**32**/33
La Biblioteca /**50**
la bibliotecaria /**50**/22
la bicicleta /**14**/5; **40**/1

el bigote /9/10; 56/21
la billetera /67/21
los billetes /20/24
la bisagra /28/5
el bizcocho /20/21
la blusa /13/6
el bobo /32/28
la boca /9/4
boca de riego /17/4
la bocina /29/20
la bodega /42/8
la bola de nieve /27/6
el bolardo /42/14
el boleto /41/7
la bolsa /20/6; 57/7; 67/2
la bolsa de compras /67/18
la bolsa de dormir /35/3
la bolsa para emparedados /67/4
la bolsa plástica /67/3
el bolsillo /11/16
el bolso /13/4
la bomba /40/16; 45/24
la bomba de aire /39/9
la bomba de gasolina /39/8
el bombardero /45/23
el bombero /17/1
la bombilla /31/13
el bombillo /31/13
bonita /75/9a
la boquilla de manguera /17/19
el borde /69/4
el borrador /18/3
borrascosa /75/4b
el bosque /34/8, 9
la bóta /10/18; 13/3; 17/6
la bota de lluvia /10/12
el bote de basura /15/27; 21/13; 30/9; 67/12
el bote de remar /43/6
la botella /32/33; 51/1; 67/5
la botella de cerveza /51/1
la botella de vino /51/25; 73/5
el botiquín /33/11
el botón /11/26; 53/15
el boxeador /46/B, 11
el Boxeo /46
la boya /42/13
las bragas /12/3
el brasier /12
el brazalete /12/8
el brazo /8/21
la brida /46/5
brincar /64/21
la brocha /24/14
el broche /53/23
el broche de presión /53/27
Una Brújula /5
bueno /75/8a
el búfalo /56/8
la bufanda /11/19
el buítre /60/10
la bujía /38/35
el bulto /18/6
el buque de guerra /45/16
el buque pesquero /43/17
el burro /56/10
la butaca /29/9
el buzón /14/1; 22/4

cabalgar /65/8
el caballo /36/25; 40/21; 52/A5; 56/1
la cabecera /32/2
el cabello /8/B9
el cabestrillo /17/23
la cabeza /8/10
la cabeza del cilindro /38/36
la cabeza del martillo /25/15
la cabina telefónica /15/28
el cable /22/17; 40/4; 42/15
el cable de energía eléctrica /37/4

el caballo (de carrera) /46/2
la cabina (del piloto) /45/22
las cabras /36/24
el cacahuete /61/11
la cacerolla /30/12
el cachete /5
el cachorro /56/14
el cactus /61/31
la cadena /33/9; 40/18; 47/20
Las Cadenas Montañosas /7
la cadera /8/7, 18
caerse /64/18
el cafetero /30/20
la caja /67/15; 73/2, 10
la caja de cartón /67/1
la caja de cerillos /73/10
la caja de embalaje /67/17
la caja de fósforos /73/2
la caja de galletas /73/2
la caja para la correspondencia /21/12
la caja registradora /20/3
la cajade píldoras /17/29
el cajón /32/18; 76/10, 11
el cajón para los jugetes /32/18
la cajuela /38/2
la cajera /20/2
la calabaza /62/7
la calavera /8/1; 38/4; 40/30
el calcetín /10/6
la calculadora /21/3
el calendario /18/20; 21/17; 70/11
caliente /74/15a
la calle /15/31
calmado /75/4a
los calzoncillos /10/5
la cama /17/19; 32/1
el camaleón /59/3
la cámara /52/25
la camarera /44/7
el camarero /51/22; 54/11
el camarote /43/1
el camello /56/6
la camilla /17/32
caminar /65/24
el camino /27/18; 34/17
el camión /14/14; 15/24; 39/11
el camión de bomberos /17/7
el camión de carga /39/14
el camión de pasajeros /39/17
el camión petrolero /39/19
el camión tractor /39/21
el camión de transporte /39/12
el camión de volteo /23/22
la camioneta /14/13; 38/40; 39/22
la camisa /11/1; 13/15
la camiseta /10/4
el camisón /12/5
el camisón de dormir /32/27
el Campamento /35/1
la campana /17/10
la campanilla /40/2
la campiña /34/13
el campo /34; 34/13; 36/8; 47/6
la caña de azúcar /63/9
la caña de pescar /48/19
el canal de desagüe /26/16
el canario /60/18
la canasta /20/7; 67/14
la canasta de frutas /30/10
la cancha /47/6; 48/23
la cancha de ténis /48/23
las candilejas /50/13
la cañería /23/9
el cangrejo /58/17
el canguro /57/6
la canoa /43/9
el cañón /45/6, 14
el cantante /49/24
cantar /65/14

cantidad /72; 73
La Cantina /51
la cantinera /51/18
el cantinero /51/19
la capa de agua /11/12
el caparazón /58/14
el capitán /44/5
la capota /38/26
la cápsula espacial /4/19
el capullo /62/25
La Cara /9
lo carabina /45/2
el caracol /58/13
el carámbano /27/8
la carátula /19/5; 70/4
la carátula del relog /70/4
el carbón /37/9
La Cárcel /16
el carcelero /16/13
la carga /42/6
cargar /64/3
la carnada /48/22
la carne /20/13
el carnicero /54/2
la carpa /35/1
la carpeta /29/22
la carpeta de papeles /18/18
el carpintero /54/3
la carrera de caballos /46
el carrete /53/8
la carretera /15/31; 23/24; 34/18; 77/6, 7, 9
el carrete (de hilo) /73/9
la carretilla /23/24; 27/27
el carril exterior /39/5
el carril interior /39/6
el carrito /20/1
el carrito del bebé /15/17
el carro /15/30; 38; 39/16
la carta /51/24
el cartapacio /21/18
las cartas /52
la cartera /13/4; 67/21
el cartero /22/5
el cartucho /45/11
la casa /26; 36/7
la casa del rancho /36/7
la casa remolcable /39/13
la cáscara /61/3, 6, 18
el casco /17/2; 40/27; 47/2
la caseta de señales /41/23
la casita de campo /35/8
el castillo de arena /35/23
las cataratas /34/4
el catre de baño /32/32
el caz /36/17
cavar /64/10
la cazuela /30/12
la cebolla /62/13
la cebra /57/24
el cedro /63/23
la celda /16/15
la ceja /9/16
el cemento /23/16
el cenicero /29/29; 51/10
la ceniza /51/9
el centímetro /53/2
la central eléctrica /37/3
el centro /68/20; 47/15
el cepillo /12/20; 31/10; 32/21
el cepillo del carpintero /25/2
el cepillo de dientes /33/17
el cepillo de a feitar /33/16
el cepillo de rasurar /33/16
el cepillo de uñas /33/20
el cepillo para pelo /32/21
la cerca /27/17; 36/10
cerca /76/15
cerca de la silla /76/15
el cerdo /56/3

cerebro /**9**/21
cereza /**61**/7
cerillo /**51**/6
s cerillos /**51**/5
cerveza de barril /**51**/16
errado /**74**/4a
cerradura de seguridad /**28**/3
errar /**65**/13
cerrojo /**28**/4
césped /**26**/21; **27**/19
cesto /**20**/7; **46**/15; **67**/14
cesto para la ropa sucia /**33**/28
cielo /**27**/10; **29**/1
encias /**19**
cienpiés /**58**/22
cierre /**53**/22
cigarrillo /**51**/8
cigarro /**51**/8
cilindro /**68**/25
cima /**34**/4
s cimientos /**23**/10
cincel /**24**/4
cine /**50**; **50**/17
cinta métrica /**53**/2
cinta de zapato /**11**/9
cinta para medir /**53**/25
cintura /**8**/16
cinturón /**10**/16
cinturón de seguridad /**38**/24
círculo /**39**/4
círculo Antártico /**5**/6
Círculo Artico /**5**/2
os Círculos /**68**
circunferencia /**68**/18
ciruela /**61**/23
cisne /**60**/17
cisterna /**37**/1
Ciudad /**14, 15**
clarinete /**49**/1
aro /**75**/11a
clavícula /**8**/2
clavijal /**31**/15
clavo /**25**/11
cliente /**20**/5; **51**/23
cloche /**38**/20
closet /**32**/14
cobertizo /**27**/26
cobertizo para herramientas /**26**/20
cobija /**32**/6
coche /**15**/17; 30; 38; **39**/16
coche deportivo /**39**/18
coco /**61**/9
cocodrilo /**59**/1
cochina /**56**/3
a Cocina /**30**; **30**/1
codo /**8**/23
oger /**64**/4
cohete /**4**/16
cohete teledirigido /**45**/4
cojín /**29**/10
col /**62**/11
cola /**56**/23; **58**/7
colcha /**32**/7
colchon /**32**/8
colegio /**18**
colibrí /**60**/27
coliflor /**62**/10
colina /**34**/10
colmillo /**57**/23
collar /**12**/10; **72**/8
comandante /**44**/5
combustible /**37**/9
omer /**64**/17
cometa /**4**/1; **35**/30
comida de lata /**20**/16
comisaria /**16**/4
conmutador /**21**/15
compartimiento de pasajeros /**41**/5
compás /**18**/11

la cómoda /**32**/16
la concha /**35**/27; **58**/14
conducir /**64**/15
el conductor /**54**/12
el conejo /**56**/20
el congelador /**20**/14
El Congo /**7**/50
El Conjunto /**49**
el cono /**63**/21; **68**/23
La Constelación /**4**/2
una Construcción /**23**
el contador /**19**/4
Los Continentes /**6**
contra /**76**/8
contra la pared /**76**/8
el convertible /**38**/38
la coraza /**59**/5
el corazón /**9**/23
la corbata /**11**/4
el corcho /**51**/26
la corcholata /**51**/2
el cordel /**22**/20; **73**/5
el cordel de ropa /**73**/5
el cordero /**36**/30
el cordón /**11**/9; **22**/20; **31**/12
el cordón del teléfono /**28**/21
el corral /**36**/5
el corralón /**36**/6
cortante /**74**/2b
cortar /**64**/8; **66**/23
cortar leña /**66**/23
La Corte de justicia /**16**
la corteza /**61**/18; **63**/17
la cortina /**26**/14; **29**/7, 8
la cortina de la bañera /**33**/31
las cortinas /**50**/6
corto /**74**/16b
la correa /**10**/16; **11**/22
el Correo /**22**
correr /**65**/8, 9
coser /**65**/11
la costa /**5**/11
la costilla /**8**/5
la costura /**53**; **53**/3
la costurera /**54**/10
la cotorra /**60**/20
el craneo /**8**/1
la crema /**12**/17; **33**/15
la crema de cara /**12**/17
la cresta /**60**/12
la crin /**36**/26
la crisálida /**59**/28
los cristales /**19**/17
el cruce /**14**/15
el cruce (paso) de peatones /**14**/2
el crucero /**43**/1
cruzando /**77**/7
el cuaderno /**8**/15; **21**/23
el cuadrante /**19**/5
el cuadrilátero /**46**/13
Los Cuadriláteros /**68C**
El Cuadrilongo /**68**
la cuadrilla /**72**/2
la cuadrilla de trabajadores /**72**/7
el cuadro /**76**/3
una cuarta parte /**69**/14
Cuartel de Bomberos /**17**
el cuartel de policía /**16**/4
el cuarto /**33**
un cuarto /**69**/14
el cuarto de proyección /**50**/14
el cuarto menguante /**4**/14
la cubeta /**31**/19; **35**/24
la cubierta /**43**/19
el cubo /**31**/19; **35**/24; **68**/24
la cubrecama /**32**/7
la cucaracha /**59**/14
la cuchara /**30**/32

la cuchara para la medicina /**17**/31
la cuchilla /**24**/5
el cuchillo /**30**/31
la cuenta /**51**/33
el cuello /**8**/11; **11**/2; **76**/6
la cuerda /**48**/20
la cuerda para colgar ropa /**27**/28
las cuerdas /**46**/14; **49**/5
el cuerno /**56**/9, 12; **57**/26
el cuerno inglés /**49**/14
El Cuerpo /**8**
El Cuerpo Humano /**8; 9**
el cuervo /**60**/33
el cuezo /**23**/18
la cueneta /**14**/9
la cuna /**32**/26
cuñada /**71**/8
el cupé /**38**/39
la cúspide /**34**/3

el chaleco /**11**/5
la chancleta /**12**/6
la chaqueta /**10**/7, 19; **11**/27; **13**/7
la chapa /**38**/28
el chapulín /**59**/12
la charca /**34**/19
el cheque postal /**22**/18
chico /**74**/1b
el chícharo /**62**/3
la chimenea /**26**/2; **29**/4; **37**/7; **42**/9; **43**/21
la china /**61**/16
la chiringa /**35**/30
el chofer /**40**/25; **54**/12
el chucho /**28**/17; **31**/17
el chupaflor /**60**/27
el chupete /**32**/28
el chupón /**32**/28, 34

La Damas /**12; 13;** 52
El Danubio /**7**/47
danzar /**64**/9
dar /**66**/11
dar cuerda /**66**/3
dar vuelta /**66**/10
el dátil /**61**/10
de /**77**/3
debajo /**76**/17
débil /**75**/6b
el decorado /**50**/4
el dedal /**53**/5
el dedo /**8**/30
el dedo del pie /**9**/41
la defensa /**38**/6
la defensa derecha /**47**/9
la defensa extrema derecha /**47**/12
la defensa izquierda /**47**/11
la defensa trasera /**47**/10
el defensor de línea /**47**/21
dejar atrás /**66**/13
el delfín /**57**/3
delgado /**74**/10b; **75**/15B
el delta /**5**/9
el dentista /**17**/16
dentro /**76**/9
dentro del cajón /**76**/9
el deoducto /**37**/12
el dependiente /**20**/8; **55**/9
los deportes /**46; 47**
deportes de invierno /**47**
el depósito /**37**/1, 14
derecho /**74**/5b
el desagüe /**14**/10; **26**/17; **33**/5
el descapotable /**38**/38
desde /**77**/3
desgarrar /**65**/21
El desierto Arabe /**7**/43
Los Desiertos /**7**
el deslizador /**47**/29
desordenado /**75**/7b
despedir /**66**/1

el destapador de botellas /**51**/7
el destornillador /**24**/7
el detergente /**20**/28
detrás /**76**/16
detrás de la silla /**76**/16
la diagonal /**68**/15
el diámetro /**68**/19
la diapositiva /**52**/30
dibujar /**64**/12
el diente /**9**/12
diez /**70**/9, 10;
difícil /**74**/12b
el dique /**37**/2; **42**/12
la dirección /**22**/11
la direccional /**38**/5
la dirección de retorno /**22**/12
el director de orquesta /**49**/10
el disco /**28**/20; **29**/21
el disparador /**45**/13
disparar /**65**/12
el distribuidor /**38**/34
diverter /**33**/7
dividido por /**69**/18
el dobladillo /**53**/4
doblar /**66**/4, 10
el doblez /**11**/18
el doctor /**17**/21; **55**/8
dormir /**66**/19
El Dormitorio /**32**
la ducha /**33**/4
el durazano /**61**/19
los durmientes /**41**/25
duro /**74**/12b, 13b

el eclipse /**4**/10
el Ecuador /**5**/4
el edificio de apartamentos /**15**/18
el edificio de oficinas /**15**/19
La Educación /**18; 19**
El Ejército /**45**
el elástico /**53**/7
el electricista /**55**/2
el elefante /**57**/21
el elevador de horquilla /**42**/17
La Elipse /**68**
la embocadura /**49**/23
el embrague /**38**/20
el empeine /**9**/39
el empleado de banco /**54**/4
el empleado de correos /**22**/1
empujar /**65**/6
en /**76**/10; **77**/8
la enagua /**12**/2
el encaje /**53**/9
el encargado de la gasolinera /**39**/10
el encendedor /**51**/14
el encendido /**38**/14
el enchufe /**31**/15, 16
el enchufle /**31**/15, 16
encima /**76**/13; **77**/1
encima de los árboles /**77**/1
encima de lamesa /**76**/13
el encimo /**63**/10
en el cajón /**76**/10
en el /**76**/10
La Energía Eléctrica /**37**
la enfermera /**17**/25; **55**/10
la engrapadora /**21**/7
el enjambre (de abejas) /**72**/16
en la esquina /**77**/8
el enrizador /**12**/22
la ensenada /**5**/8
entre /**77**/5, 12
entre los automóviles /**77**/12
entre los árboles /**77**/5
El Entretenimiento /**49**
Los Enuases /**67**
el envase /**33**/15
la envoltura plástica /**67**/10

el equipaje /**44**/4
el equipo /**72**/15
el equipo de jugadores /**47c; 72**/15
el erizo /**56**/26
la escala /**33**/24
escalar /**64**/5
la escalera /**17**/11; **23**/5; **28**/12
la escalera extensible /**17**/8
el escalón /**28**/11
el escalón peldaño /**23**/6
las escamas /**58**/9; **59**/7
el escaporate /**15**/21
el escarabajo /**59**/13
el escenario /**50**/1
el escorpión /**58**/27
escribir /**66**/2
escribir a máquina /**66**/21
el escritorio /**50**/24
escuchar /**65**/1
la escuela /**18**
la esencia /**12**/15
el esmalte de uñas /**12**/14
el Espacio /**4**
la espalda /**8**/15; **69**/6
la espanta pájaros /**36**/13
el espejo /**32**/13; **40**/3
el espejo retrovisar /**38**/1
los espejuelos /**11**/23
la espina dorsal /**8**/6
la esponja /**33**/26
las esposas /**16**/8
el esqueleto /**8**
el esquiador /**47**/25
el esquí /**47**/26
la esquina /**69**/3; **77**/8
el estabilizador /**43**/4
el establo /**36**/4
el establo para reses /**36**/3
la estación /**41**/13
el estacionamiento /**15**/29
la estación de energía eléctrica /**37**/6
la estación de servicio /**39**/7
la estación de tren /**14**/3
el estadio /**47**
la estampilla /**22**/9
el estanque /**34**/19
el estanque de corral /**36**/9
el estante /**20**/15; **30**/16
el estante de libros /**50**/25
el estante para libros /**21**/24
estar acostado /**65**/3
el este /**5**
el esternon /**8**/4
el estetoscopio /**17**/22
el estómago /**8**/17
el estrado /**49**/13
estrecho /**75**/1a
La Estrella /**4**/5
el estibador /**54**/6
el estribo /**46**/7
el estuario /**5**/10
el estuche /**32**/24
la estudiante /**18**/5
la estufa /**30**/1
la etiqueta /**22**/21
Europa /**6**/3
la excavadora /**23**/20
excavar /**64**/10
el excusado /**33**/8
la extensión eléctrica /**24**/10
el extinguidor de incendios /**17**/5
la extrema izquierda /**47**/18

fácil /**74**/12a
el faisán /**60**/14
la falda /**13**/8

el farol /**15**/22
el farol cola /**38**/4; **40**/30
el farol delantero /**38**/29; **40**/5
el farol trasero /**40**/30
Las Fases de la Luna /**4**
la faz (del reloj) /**70**/4
La Fecha /**70**
feliz /**74**/11a
feo /**75**/9b
el fichero /**21**/26; **50**/23
Las figuras Sólidas /**68**
la Finca /**36**
el fiscal /**16**/23
el flamenco /**60**/8
el flamingo /**60**/8
la flor /**27**/20
Las Flores /**62**
la flonsta /**55**/5
la flota (de barcos) /**72**/4
Fluvial /**43**
la foca /**57**/9
el foco /**31**/13
el fondo /**12**
la formación en T /**47**/19
el formón /**24**/4
el fósforo /**51**/6
los fósforos /**51**/5
la foto /**52**/22
la fotografiá /**52**/22
el fotógrafo /**55**/4
la fracción /**69**/22
el frasco /**19**/16
el frasco de medicina /**17**/30
la frazada /**32**/6
el fregadero /**30**/7
el freno /**38**/19, 22; **40**/14, 33; **46**/6
el freno de mano /**38**/19
la frente /**9**/8
el frente /**69**/7
frente a /**76**/7
la fresa /**61**/21
el frijol /**62**/1
frío /**74**/15b
la frisa /**32**/6
la fronda /**61**/33
fruncir el ceño /**66**/14
las frutas /**20**/17; **30**/11; **57**
el fuego /**17**/12; **29**/6
fuerte /**75**/6a
La Fuerza Aérea /**45**
las Fuerzas Armadas /**45**
La Fuerza Eléctrica /**37**
la funda /**32**/4
la furgoneta /**39**/22
el fuselaje /**44**/10
El Fútbol /**47**

el gabetero /**32**/16
el gabinete /**30**/6
los gajos /**61**/17
la galaxia /**4**/3
la galería /**50**/9
las galletas /**20**/26
las galletitas /**20**/20
la gallina /**36**/33
el gallo /**36**/34
el gancho /**28**/10
El Ganges /**7**/52
el ganso /**60**/25
el garaje /**26**/6
la garganta /**8**/12
la garra /**60**/3
el garrote /**16**/7
la garza /**60**/15
la gasolinera /**39**/7
gatear /**64**/6
el gatillo /**45**/13
el gatito /**56**/16
el gato /**56**/15

el gavilán /**60**/6
la gaviota /**60**/21
geometría /**68**
el giraso /**62**/27
el giro /**22**/18
el globo ocular /**9**/15
El Globo Terráqueo /**5**
El Gobi /**7**/44
el Golfo de Alaska /**6**/15
el Golfo de Bengala /**6**/28
el Golfo de Guinea /**6**/19
el Golfo de México /**6**/17
el Golfo de Persa /**6**/26
los Golfos /**6**
la golondrina /**60**/22
golpear /**66**/5
la goma /**38**/8; **40**/11
la goma de pegar /**18**/13
gordo /**74**/10a
el gorila /**57**/14
la gorra /**46**/9
el gorrión /**60**/28
las gotas de lluvia /**27**/4
la gradería /**47**/5
la grama /**27**/19
la granada de mano /**45**/9
grande /**74**/1a
la Granja /**36**
el granjero /**36**/15
el grano de cacao /**63**/4
el grano de café /**63**/5
el grillo /**59**/11
la grúa /**23**/1; **42**/4
grueso /**75**/15a
el grupo /**72**/11
grupo de música popular /**49**
el grupo de turistas /**72**/11
la guagua /**39**/17
el guajalote /**60**/16
el guante /**11**/20; **46**/12; **48**/3
el guardabarros /**40**/10
el guardabosque derecho /**47**/14
el guardabosque izquierdo /**47**/16
el guarda espalda /**47**/8
el guardafangos /**40**/10
el guardafrenos /**41**/10
el guardavía /**41**/22
la guía telefónica /**28**/22
el guía /**40**/6
los guijarros /**35**/28
el guineo /**61**/5
a guitarra /**49**/26
a guitarra eléctrica /**49**/26
el gusano /**58**/21

a habichuela /**62**/1
a habitación /**76**/1
el hacha /**24**/6; **25**/7
hacia /**77**/10
alar /**65**/5
el halcón /**60**/6
el hangar /**44**/21
el haz /**72**/2
el haz de varas /**72**/2
a hebilla /**10**/17
l helado /**35**/17
l helecho /**61**/32
a hélice del aeroplano /**44**/18
l helicóptero /**44**/15
a hembra /**53**/23
l henil /**36**/1
l heno /**36**/2
ermana /**71**/5
ermana política /**71**/8
ermano /**71**/5
ermano político /**71**/8
ermosa /**75**/92
l herradura /**36**/27
as Herramientas /**25**

hervir /**66**/22
el hibisco /**62**/24
el hidrante /**17**/4
la hierba /**26**/21
el hígado /**9**/25
el higo /**61**/29
hija /**71**/3
hijos /**71**/2
hilar /**66**/16
la hilera (de casas) /**72**/14
hilo /**53**/8
el Himalaya /**7**/40
el hipopótamo /**57**/20
la hipotenusa /**68**/12
el Hoang Ho /**7**/54
el hocico /**56**/4; **58**/8
el Hockey /**46**
la hoja /**63**/15
la hoja de papel /**18**/17
las hojas /**24**/15
el hombre de nieve /**27**/7
Los Hombres /**10**; **11**
el hombro /**8**/13
el hongo /**62**/14
la hora /**70**
el horario /**41**/15
el horizonte /**42**/1
la hormiga /**59**/17
la hornilla /**30**/4
la hornilla para acampar /**35**/5
el horno /**30**/2
la horquilla /**27**/25
el hotel /**35**/7
hueco /**75**/14b
las huellas /**16**/A12
las huellas digitales /**16**/A11
el huerto /**36**/12
los huevos /**20**/11
el humo /**17**/13

Identificación /**16**
la ignición /**38**/14
igual /**69**/19
la ilustración /**52**/20
el imán /**19**/19
el impermeable /**11**/12
el incendio /**17**/12
Incendios /**17**
el índice de direcciones /**21**/26
el Indico /**6**/13
El Indo /**7**/51
el inodoro /**33**/8
Los Insectos /**59**   ·
el inspector /**41**/16
el inspector de boletos /**41**/6
la instalación petrolera /**37**/10
La Instrucción /**18**; **19**
los intestinos /**9**/27
la iris /**9**/20
la isla /**5**/12

la jota de trébol /**52**/11
la jaba /**20**/6
el jabón /**33**/27
el jabón de polvo /**31**/18
el jardín de flores /**27**/21
la jardinera /**26**/13
el jardinero /**55**/3
el jardinero del centro /**48**/16
el jardinero derecho /**48**/17
el jardinero izquierdo /**48**/15
la jarra /**51**/3
el jarro /**67**/6
el jeep /**45**/5
la jirafa /**57**/15
el jitomate /**62**/15
el jockey /**46**/1
la joroba /**56**/7
joven /**75**/2a

el joyero /**32**/24
el Judo /**46**
el juego /**32**/20; **52**; **52**/1
el juego de barajas /**52**/10
el juego de damas /**52**/9
el juez /**16**/22
el jugador /**46**/24
el jugador con el saque /**48**/25
el jugador de primera base /**48**/10
el jugador de segunda base /**48**/11
el jugador de tercera base /**48**/13
el juguete /**32**/19
los juguetes /**32**/18
la juntas /**11**/25
junto /**76**/14
el jurado /**16**/17

el Kalahari /**7**/42

el labio /**9**/13
el laboratorio /**19**
el lado /**68**/13; **69**/5
los ladrillos /**23**/8
la lagartija /**59**/9
el lago /**5**/13; **34**/5
lamer /**64**/25
la lámpara /**17**/18; **29**/26
la lana /**53**/19
la lancha /**43**/15
la lancha de motor /**35**/34; **43**/11
la langosta /**59**/10
la langosta de mar /**58**/12
el lanzador /**48**/10
el lapicero /**21**/27
el lápiz /**18**/8
el lápiz de labios /**12**/18
el largo /**69**/11
largo /**74**/16a
la lata /**30**/22; **67**/7
la lata de cerveza /**51**/4
la lata de pintura /**24**/17
la latitud /**5**/15
el latón /**15**/27
el lavado /**33**/12
la lavadora eléctrica /**31**/4
el lavamano /**33**/12
lavar /**65**/25
la leche /**20**/10
el lechón /**56**/3
la lechosa /**61**/25
la lechuga /**62**/12
la lechuza /**60**/7
la lectura /**52**
leer /**65**/7
las legumbres /**62**
lejos /**77**/11
la lengua /**9**/14; **59**/8
el leño /**63**/18
los lentes /**11**/23; **19**/10; **52**/26
lento /**74**/9b
el león /**57**/16
el leopardo /**57**/18
les /**69**/19
levantar /**66**/8
La Ley /**16**
la libélula /**59**/19
el librero /**29**/16
la libreta /**21**/23
el libro /**18**/14; **52**/15
el libro de citas /**21**/5
el licor /**51**/17
ligar /**65**/23
la lima /**24**/2
la lima de uñas /**12**/11
el limón /**61**/14
el limpiaparabrisas /**38**/11
limpio /**74**/3a
la línea curva /**68**/7
la línea de servicio /**48**/26

la línea espiral /**68**/1
la línea foul /**48**/14
la línea perpendicular /**68**/4
la línea recta /**68**/2
la línea zig-zag /**68**/6
las Líneas /**68**
las líneas paralelas /**68**/5
la linterna /**16**/9
el lirio acuático /**62**/26
liso /**75**/5b
el listón /**53**/24
el litchi /**61**/26
liviano /**75**/12a
el lobo /**57**/11
la loceta /**33**/29
la locomotora /**41**/3
el locutor /**54**/15
la loma /**34**/10
el lomo /**52**/18
la longitud /**5**/14
el loro /**60**/20
las luces /**47**/7
la Lucha /**46**
los luchadores /**46**/22
La Luna /**4**/6
la luna creciente /**4**/11
la luna llena /**4**/13
la luna nueva /**4**/11
la lupa /**16**/10
la luz /**28**/16
la luz indicadora /**38**/5
la luz trasera /**38**/4
la llama /**17**/13; **56**/5
el llamador /**28**/2
la llanta /**38**/8; **40**/11
la llave /**24**/13
la llave de agua caliente /**33**/2
la llave de aqua fría /**33**/3
la llave de cerveza /**51**/20
la llave inglesa /**24**/9, 13
lleno /**74**/8b
llevar /**64**/3
llorar /**64**/7
la lluvia /**27**/3

la maceta /**27**/24
el macho /**53**/23
el macizo /**27**/21
madre /**71**/4
la maestra /**18**/1; **55**/11
los mahones /**10**/14; **13**/14
el malecón /**42**/2
la maleta /**38**/2; **67**/19
el maletín /**11**/28; **67**/20
malo /**75**/8b
la mamadera /**32**/34
la mampara /**35**/18
la manada de ovejas /**72**/6
las mancuernas /**11**/25
la mandíbula /**9**/9
el mandril /**57**/13
la manecilla de la hora /**70**/2
manejar /**64**/15
la manga /**11**/7; **33**/9
el mango /**33**/9; **61**/15
el mango de martillo /**25**/16
la manguera /**17**/3
el maní /**61**/11
la mano /**8**/27; **19**/6
la mano de mortero /**19**/20
el manojo (de varas) /**72**/2
la manta /**32**/6
el mantel /**51**/31
el mantel individual /**30**/30
el mantis /**59**/15
el manubrio /**40**/6
la manzana /**61**/1
el mapa /**5**; **18**/19
el mapo /**31**/5

la máquina /**15**/30; **38**; **39**/16; **41**/3
la máquina de afeitar /**33**/13
la máquina de coser /**53**/1
la máquina de escribir /**21**/21
la máquina de lavar platos /**30**/24
la máquina de sacar cópias /**21**/14
la máquina de sumar /**21**/8
la maquinilla /**21**/21
el maquinista /**41**/2
la maraquita /**32**/30
el marco de la ventana /**26**/9
el Mar Arabe /**6**/27
el Mar Báltico /**6**/21
el Mar Caribe /**6**/18
el Mar Caspio /**6**/24
el Mar Mediterráneo /**6**/22
el Mar Negro /**6**/23
el Mar Rojo /**6**/25
el Mar de Bering /**7**/35
el Mar de China Meridional /**7**/31
el Mar de China Oriental /**7**/32
el Mar de Coral /**6**/29
el Mar de Tasmania /**6**/30
el Mar de Ujostk /**7**/34
el Mar del Japón /**7**/33
el Mar del Norte /**6**/20
los Mares /**6**
la margarita /**62**/18
marido /**71**/1
la marina /**45**
el marinero /**55**/15
la mariposa /**59**/25
marítimo /**43**
el martillo /**25**/14
el martin pescador /**60**/30
más /**69**/15
más allá de /**77**/2
la máscara protector /**48**/2
el mástil /**43**/3
el matraz /**19**/16
el mazo cuadrado /**25**/1
la mazorca de maíz /**63**/1
el mecánico /**54**/5
los mecánicos /**10**/14; **13**/14
la mecanógrafa /**54**/9
el mechero de Bunsen /**19**/12
la media /**10**/6; **13**/12
la media luna /**4**/12
las medias panties /**12**/4
el médico /**17**/21; **55**/8
Las Medidas /**69**
la medida para las bebidas /**51**/34
el medidor de gasolina /**38**/13
la medusa /**59**/11
la mejilla /**9**/5
el Mekong /**7**/53
la melena /**57**/17
el melocotón /**61**/19
menos /**69**/17; **70**/9, 10
el mentón /**9**/6
el menú /**51**/24
la mesa /**30**/26; **46**/21; **76**/14, 17
la mesa de noche /**32**/9
el mesero /**51**/22; **54**/11
la meseta /**34**/1
la mesita /**29**/23, 25
el metro /**15**/23; **24**/12; **40**/23
el mezclador /**36**/16
la mezcladora de cemento /**23**/21
el micrófono /**49**/25
el microscopio /**19**/9
el minero /**54**/7
el minutero /**70**/1
el mirasol /**62**/27
el mirlo /**60**/32
El Misisipi /**7**/45
una mitad /**69**/12
el mocasín /**10**/10
la mochila /**18**/6; **35**/4

el modelo /**53**/20
la modista /**54**/10
el mofile /**38**/7; **39**/35
mojado /**74**/7a
el moledor de pimienta /**51**/29
las monedas /**20**/25
el mono /**57**/12
la montaña /**34**/2
las Montañas Roqueñas /**7**/36
montar a caballo /**65**/8
los Montes Urales /**7**/39
el montón /**72**/9, 11
el montón de piedras /**72**/9
la morsa /**24**/8
el mortero /**19**/21
la mosca /**59**/23
el mosquito /**59**/20
el mostrador /**22**/3; **30**/8; **51**/15
mostrador de la caja /**20**/4
la motocicleta /**14**/16; **39**/20
la motoneta /**14**/16; **40**/29
el motor /**38**/31
el motor fuera de borda /**43**/12
el motor de reacción /**44**/12
mover /**65**/18
el mozo /**51**/22
la muchedumbre /**72**/3
el muelle /**42**/5, 12
mujer /**71**/1
las muletas /**17**/26
multiplicado por /**69**/16
El Mundo /**5**; 6
la muñeca /**8**/25; **32**/31
la muralla /**35**/10
el murciélago /**56**/25
el músculo /**9**/31
La Música /**49**
el músico /**49**/3
el muslo /**8**/33

el nadador /**35**/35
nadar /**65**/20
las nalgas /**8**/19
la naranja /**61**/16
el narciso /**62**/17
naregar /**65**/10
la nariz /**9**/2
la navaja /**24**/5; **33**/14
el navegante /**45**/26
el negativo /**52**/23
el neumático /**38**/8; **40**/11
la nevera /**30**/5
el nido /**60**/29
nieta /**71**/12
nieto /**71**/12
la nieve /**27**/5
El Níger /**7**/49
El Nilo /**7**/48
Los Niños /**10**; **11**
Las Niñas /**12**; **13**
el nivel /**23**/19
Nombres /**72**; **73**
el nopal /**61**/31
el nordeste /**5**
noreste /**5**
el noroeste /**5**
el norte /**5**
Norteamérica /**6**/1
el nubarrón /**27**/2
la nube de tormenta /**27**/2
nuera /**71**/7
nuestro /**4**
las nueve cincuenta /**70**/10
las nueve en punto /**70**/5
las nueve y cuarenta y cinco /**70**/9
las nueve y cuarto /**70**/7
las nueve y diez /**70**/6
las nueve y media /**70**/8
las nueve y quince /**70**/7

las nueve y treinta /**70**/8
nuevo /**75**/3a
la nuez /**61**/27
el número del andén /**41**/21

Una Obra /**23**
el obrero /**23**/14
el obturador de aire /**38**/15
Los Océanos /**6**
el oculista /**55**/14
Las Ocupaciones /**54; 55**
el oeste /**5**
la oficina /**21**
oir /**65**/1
el ojal /**53**/16
el ojo /**9**; **9**/1
la ola /**35**/33
el oleaje (espuma de ola) /**35**/32
la olla /**30**/12
el omnoplato /**8**/3
la operadora /**21**/16
la órbita /**4**/9
ordenado /**75**/7a
la oreja /**9**/3
los órganos internos /**9**
La Orquesta /**49**
la orquídea /**62**/21
la orquilla /**13**/13
la oruga /**59**/27
oscuro /**75**/11b
el osito de peluche /**32**/29
el oso /**57**/8
el ostión /**58**/16
la ostra /**58**/16
otros /**58**
El Ovalo /**68**/6
la oveja /**36**/29
el ovillo de hilo /**73**/1
el ovillo de lana /**73**/1

el paciente /**17**/20
el Pacífico del Norte /**6**/9
el Pacífico del Sur /**6**/10
padre /**71**/4
la página /**52**/19
la paja /**51**/12
Los Pájaros /**60**
la pala /**23**/13; **35**/25
la palanca de velocidades /**38**/21; **40**/38
el palco /**50**/10
la palma /**8**/28
la palmera /**63**/19
el palo /**46**/18; **63**/18
el palo de esquiar /**47**/27
la paloma /**60**/31
la paloma torcaz /**60**/24
el pan /**20**/19; **73**/6
el panadero /**55**/7
el pañal /**32**/36
la panera /**30**/15
las pantaletas /**12**/3
los pantalones /**10**/8; **11**/17, 29
los pantalones de equitación /**46**/8
la pantalla /**12**/9; **29**/27; **50**/18; **52**/27
las pantimedias /**12**/4
la pantorrilla /**8**/35
la pantufla /**10**/3; **12**/6
el pañuelo /**13**/9
los pañuelos desechables /**32**/23
la papa /**62**/6
el papalote /**35**/30
las papas /**20**/27
la papaya /**61**/25
papel /**67**/2
el papel carbón /**21**/20
el papel de aluminio /**67**/11
el papel de lija /**24**/3
el papel higiénico /**33**/10
el papel secante /**21**/4

el papote /**51**/12
el paquete /**22**/19; **73**/10
el paquete de cigarrillos /**73**/10
el paquete de cigarros /**73**/10
el parabrisas /**38**/10
el paracaídas /**45**/25
el parachoques /**41**/29
la parada de autobus /**15**/25
el paraguas /**11**/24
parar (se) /**65**/17
la pared /**26**/3; **29**/2; /**76**/4, 5
la parilla /**30**/3
el párpado /**9**/17
el parque /**14**/11
el parque de pelota /**48**
la parra /**61**/13
la parte /**69**/1, 2
la parte de abajo /**69**/2
la parte de arriba /**69**/1
la parte superior del brazo /**8**/22
la partitura /**49**/12
el pasadizo /**42**/10
el pasador de cortina /**33**/30
el pasaje /**40**/24; **41**/7
el pasajero /**40**/26
los pasajeros /**41**/19
el pasaporte /**44**/3
pasar /**66**/13
Los Pasatiempos /**52**
el paseo /**35**/9
el pasillo /**28**; **50**/21
el paso subterráneo /**39**/3
el paso superior /**39**/2
la pasta /**52**/16
la pasta de dientes /**33**/21
el pastel /**20**/24
el pasto /**26**/21
la pata con membrana entre /**60**/9
    los dedos
patear /**64**/22
el patín /**47**/31
el patinador /**47**/30
el patito /**26**/5; 27; **36**/31
el pato /**36**/32
el patrón /**53**/20
la patrulla /**16**/5
el patrullero /**16**/5
el pavo /**60**/6
el pavo real /**60**/11
el payaso /**54**/13
los peces /**58**
el pecho /**8**/14
el pedal /**40**/17, 37; **49**/17
el pedal de arranque /**40**/36
el pedazo /**73**/4, 8
el pedazo de bizcocho /**73**/8
el pedazo de carne /**73**/4
pegar /**66**/5
peinar /**66**/12
el peine /**12**/19; **32**/22
la peinilla /**12**/19; **32**/22
pelear /**64**/19
el pelo /**8**/9
la pelota /**46**/17
la pelota de fútbol /**47**/1
la pelota de playa /**35**/26
la pelota de tenis /**48**/28
la peluquera /**54**/1
la pelvis /**8**/7
el peón /**52**/3
la pepa /**61**/8, 20
el pepinillo /**62**/8
el pepino /**62**/8
pequeño /**74**/1b
la pera /**61**/22
el perchero /**28**/9
la perforadora /**21**/6
la perforadora de aire comprimido /**23**/23
el perfume /**12**/15

el periquito /**60**/26
el periodico /**29**/12
el periscopio /**45**/20
el perno /**25**/8
la persiana /**26**/12, 15
la persona tomando sol /**35**/13
el perrito /**56**/14
el perro /**56**/13
el perro policía /**16**/6
la pesacartas /**22**/2
pesado /**75**/12b
las pesas /**19**/3
La Pesca /**48**
el pescado /**20**/22
el pescador /**48**/18
las pestañas /**9**/18
el pétalo /**62**/20
el petrolero /**43**/18
el pez dorado /**58**/15
el pez espada /**58**/3
la pezuña /**56**/17
el piano /**49**/15
el pica de ave /**60**/19
el pichón /**60**/31
el pico /**23**/12; **60**/4
el pie /**8**/37
las piedras lisas /**35**/28
la piel /**61**/3
la pierna /**8**/32
las piezas /**52**/1
el pijama /**10**/2
la pila /**72**/12
la pila de frazadas /**72**/12
la pila de frisas /**72**/12
la pileta /**30**/7; **33**/12
el piloto /**44**/5; **45**/27
el piloto de avión /**45**/27
el piloto deslizador /**47**/28
la pimentera /**30**/40
el pimentero /**51**/30
la piña /**61**/24; **63**/21
el pinche /**12**/23
El Ping-Pong /**46**
el pinquino /**60**/13
el pino /**63**/20
el piñón /**40**/19
pintar /**65**/4
la pintora /**54**/8
la pinza /**27**/30; **58**/18
la pipeta /**19**/18
la pirámide /**68**/22
el piso /**28**/7
el piso de la carpa /**35**/2
el piso de la tienda /**35**/2
la pista /**44**/19
la pistola /**45**/10
el pito /**41**/12
la pizarra /**18**/2; **38**/12
la pizarra de puntuación /**43**/23
el pizarrón /**18**/2
la placa /**38**/28
la placa de matrícula /**38**/28
la plancha /**31**/11
la plancha del radiador /**38**/27
planchar /**66**/18
el planeador /**44**/14
el planeta /**4**/4
la planta alta /**28**/14
la planta baja /**28**/15; **50**/11
la planta del pie /**9**/40
Las Plantas /**61**; **62**; **63**
la plataforma /**41**/20
la plataforma de lanzamiento /**4**/17
el plátano /**61**/5
la platea /**50**/12
el platillo /**19**/2
los platillos /**49**/29
la platina /**19**/11
el plato /**30**/34; **48**/9; **72**/13

el plato de bocadillos /**72**/13
el plato hondo /**30**/35
la playa /**35**/11; **77**/4
el pliegue /**53**/11
el plisado /**53**/11
la pluma /**18**/9
las plumas /**60**/5
poco profundo /**74**/6b
el policía /**61**/1; **55**/13
la polilla /**59**/26
el pollito /**36**/35
el pollo /**36**/33
el polluelo /**36**/35
el Polo Norte /**5**/1
el Polo Sur /**5**/7
el polvo /**32**/37
el polvo compacto /**12**/12
el polvo dejabon /**20**/28
el polvo limpiador /**31**/9
el pomelo /**61**/30
poner /**66**/15
la popa /**43**/14
el porcentaje /**69**/20
el por ciento /**69**/20
el portaaviones /**45**/18
la portada /**52**/17
el portaequipajes /**40**/8, 34
el portaservilletas /**30**/29
la portería /**47**/4, 22
el portero /**54**/14
el portier /**29**/8
el portón /**27**/16; **41**/17
el porquimetro /**15**/23
el poste del tablero /**46**/16
el pote /**24**/17
el pote de pintura /**24**/17
el potrillo /**56**/2
la pradera /**34**/11
el prado /**34**/11
Preposiciones /**76**
la presilla /**21**/9
la presilladora /**21**/7
el preso /**16**/14
la primera base /**48**/11
primero /**75**/10a
primo /**71**/9
la proa /**43**/13
Las Profesiones /**54, 55**
la profundidad /**69**/10
profundo /**74**/6b
la proyeccionista /**50**/16
el proyectil /**45**/7
el proyector /**50**/15; **52**/29
el puente /**14**/12; **77**/2, 10, 11
el puerco /**56**/3
la puerta /**28**/1; **76**/2
la puerta de entrada /**26**/7
el pulgar /**8**/29
el pulmón /**9**/24
el pulpo /**58**/23
la pulsera /**12**/8
la puntada /**53**/17
las puntas /**41**/26
el punto decimal /**69**/21
el puño /**8**/26; **11**/3
la pupila /**9**/19
el pupitre /**18**/7

el quarterback /**47**/8
el queso /**20**/9
la quijada /**9**/9
la quilla /**43**/5
la quinta /**35**/8
el quitaso /**35**/12

el radiador /**38**/33
la radio /**29**/24; **38**/25
la radiografía /**17**/24
el radio de automóvil /**38**/25

las raíces /**63**/11
la rama /**27**/13; **63**/13
la ramita /**63**/14
las ramitas /**27**/14
el ramo /**72**/1
el ramo de flores /**72**/1
el ranchero /**36**/15
rápido /**74**/9a
la raqueta /**46**/19
la raqueta de tenis /**48**/27
la rata /**56**/22
el ratón /**56**/18
los rayos /**40**/12
el rebaño /**72**/10
el rebaño de vacas /**72**/10
La Recámara /**32**
la recepcionista /**21**/25
el receptor /**28**/19; **48**/1
el receptor auricular /**28**/19
el recibo /**20**/23
Los Recipientes /**67**
el recogedor /**31**/8
La Recreación /**46; 49; 51; 52**
Los Rectángulos /**68**
la red /**46**/20; **48**/24
la refinería /**37**/13
el reflector /**40**/20; **50**/7
el refresco /**51**/13
el refrigerador /**30**/5
la regadera /**27**/23; **33**/4
la regla /**18**/10
la regla de cálculo /**18**/16
la reina /**52**/7
la reina de díamantes /**52**/12
reirse /**64**/24
las rejas /**16**/16
la rejilla para equipaje /**41**/9
el relámpago /**27**/1
el reloj /**11**/21
el reloj despertador /**32**/25
el remo /**43**/7
el remo de la canoa /**43**/10
la remolacha /**62**/9
el remolcador /**42**/19
el reno /**56**/11
la repisa de la chimenea /**29**/5
el repollo /**62**/11
la represa /**37**/2
Los Reptiles /**59**
El Restaurante /**51**
la revista /**29**/15
las revistas /**29**/14
el revólver /**16**/2; **45**/12
revolver /**65**/18
el rey /**52**/8
el rey de corazones /**52**/13
el riachuelo /**34**/7
las riendas /**46**/4
el rifle /**45**/2
el rímel para las pestañas /**12**/13
el ring /**46**/13
el rinoceronte /**57**/25
el riñón /**9**/26
el rio /**34**/7
Los Rios /**7**
el roble /**63**/10
las rocas /**35**/29
la rodilla /**8**/34
el rodillo de pintura /**24**/15
el rolo /**12**/22
el rollo /**73**/12
el rollo de papel /**73**/12
el rollo de película /**52**/24
la romana /**33**/24
romo /**74**/2a
romper /**64**/2; **65**/21
el rompeviento /**35**/18
La Ropa /**10; 11; 12; 13**
la ropa de baño /**35**/36

la ropa lavada /**27**/29
el ropero /**32**/14
la rosa /**62**/19
la rosca /**25**/10
la rotonda de tráfico /**39**/4
el rotor /**44**/16
la rótula /**8**/8
el rótulo /**14**/7
la rueda /**40**/9
la rueda dentada /**40**/19
el ruedo /**53**/4
ruidoso /**75**/13a

la sábana /**32**/5
el sacacorchos /**51**/11
el saco /**10**/7; **11**/27; **67**/2
el saco de correspondencia /**22**/6
el safacón /**21**/13; **30**/9
el safacón de basura /**67**/12
El Sahara /**7**/41
La Sala /**29**
la sala de espera /**41**/18
una sala de hospital /**17**
las salchichas /**20**/12
el salero /**30**/39; **51**/28
el salmón /**58**/4
el saltamontes /**59**/12
saltar /**64**/21
la sandalia /**13**/17
el sapo /**58**/20
el sartén /**30**/13, 14
el satélite /**4**/18
el sauce /**63**/24
el saxofón /**49**/22
el secador de pelo /**31**/14
el secador de platos /**30**/25
la sección /**68**/21
seco /**74**/7b
la secretaria /**21**/22
el sedán /**38**/37
el segundero /**70**/3
el sello /**22**/9
el sello impreso /**22**/8
el semáforo /**14**/6
semilunio /**4**/12
la semilla /**61**/4, 8, 20
las semillas /**62**/28
el sendero /**27**/18; **34**/17
sentar (se) /**65**/15
las señales /**41**/27
Los Servicios Médicos /**17**
la servilleta /**30**/28; **51**/32
el serrucho /**25**/17
el serrucho eléctrico /**24**/11
la seta /**62**/14
el seto /**34**/14
el sien /**9**/7
la sierra /**25**/18
el silbato /**41**/12
la silla /**29**/13; **30**/27; **76**/7
la silla de montar /**36**/28; 46/3
la silla de playa /**35**/19
el sillón /**17**/15; **29**/11
sin punta /**74**/2a
el snorkel /**35**/16
el sobaco /**8**/20
sobre /**76**/12; **77**/7
el sobre /**21**/11; **22**/15
el sobre aéreo /**22**/10
la sobrecama /**32**/7
el sobrecargo /**44**/8
sobre la carretera /**77**/7
sobre la mesa /**76**/12
el sobretodo /**11**/14
sobrina /**71**/11
sobrino /**71**/11
el sofá /**29**/9
el sol /**4**/8; **27**/9
la solapa /**11**/15

solapa del sobre /**22**/16
soldado /**45**/1; **55**/12
lido /**75**/14a
sombra para ojos /**12**/16
sombrero /**11**/13
sombrero de lluvia /**11**/30
sombrilla de playa /**35**/12
sonaja /**32**/30
sonajero /**32**/30
ñar /**64**/14
nreir /**65**/16
plar /**64**/1
sorbeto /**51**/12
sortija /**12**/7
sostén /**12**/1
stener /**66**/20
stadora /**30**/18
ave /**74**/13a; **75**/5b, 13b
biendo por /**76**/5
bir /**64**/5
submarino /**45**/19
cio /**74**/3b
sud /**5**
damerica /**6**/2
sudeste /**5**
sudoeste /**5**
egra /**71**/6
egro /**71**/6
suela /**11**/10
elto /**75**/16a
suéter /**10**/15; **13**/1, 16
suétar abierto /**10**/9
Supermercado /**20**
sur /**5**
uramérica /**6**/2
surco /**36**/20
sureste /**5**
suroeste /**5**
surtidor /**39**/8

a Taberna /**51**
tabla /**29**/17; **31**/3
tabla de planchar /**31**/3
tableado /**53**/11
tablero /**30**/8; **38**/12; **52**/2
tablero de control /**45**/28
tablero de mandos /**38**/12
tablero de puntuación /**47**/23
tablilla /**24**/18; **30**/16
tablón /**23**/11
tablón de edictos/avisos /**21**/10
taburete /**32**/12; **49**/18; **51**/21
taco /**11**/11
tacón /**11**/11
aguagua /**15**/24
taladradora eléctrica /**25**/4
taladro /**17**/7; **25**/6
taladro de mano /**25**/3
taladro eléctrico /**25**/4
talón /**9**/38
n Taller /**24**
tallo /**61**/2; **62**/2, 23
tambor /**49**/30
tanque /**45**/8
tanto /**46**/25
tapa /**38**/26; **51**/2
tapete /**32**/17
tapetito /**26**/18; **28**/6
tapón /**33**/6; **38**/30
tapón de desagüe /**33**/6
tapón de la gasolina /**38**/3
taquígrafo /**16**/25
tarado /**56**/11
tarjeta postal /**22**/14
tarro /**51**/3
taxi /**14**/4; **40**/22
taximetro /**40**/22
taxista /**40**/25
taza /**30**/37; **73**/11;

la taza de cafe /**73**/11
el tazón /**73**/14
el tazón de sopa /**73**/14
el té /**63**/8
el teatro /**50**; **50**/8
el techo /**26**/1; **29**/1
las teclas /**49**/16
la teja /**23**/4
el tejido /**53**/21
la tela /**53**/13
la tela de araña /**58**/26
la telaraña /**58**/26
el teléfono /**21**/2; **28**/18
el telegrama /**22**/17
la televisión /**29**/28
el televisor /**29**/28
la temperatura /**70**
la tenaza /**25**/19
el tenedor /**27**/25; **30**/33
El Tenis /**48**
los tenis /**10**/13
el tenis de mesa /**46**
el tentáculo /**58**/24
una tercera parte /**69**/13
un tercio /**69**/13
el termo /**67**/9
el termómetro /**17**/28; **70**/12
el ternero /**36**/22
el terrón /**73**/7
el terrón de azúcar /**73**/7
el testigo /**16**/19
la tetera /**30**/17
el texto /**52**/21
tía /**71**/10
el tiburón /**58**/1
El Tiempo /**27**
la tienda /**15**/20
la tienda de campaña /**35**/1
La Tierra /**4**/7
el tiesto /**27**/24
el tigre /**57**/19
las tijeras /**53**/26
el timbre /**22**/9; **40**/2
el timón /**38**/17
la tina /**33**/1
tío /**71**/10
tirar /**66**/9
la tiza /**18**/4
la toalla /**33**/22; **35**/14
la toalla de playa /**35**/14
el toallero /**33**/23
la toallita /**33**/19
la tobera propulsora /**4**/15
el tobillo /**8**/36
el tocadiscos /**29**/19
el tocador /**32**/10
tocar /**65**/22
la toga /**16**/24
el tomacorriente /**31**/16
tomar /**64**/4, 13
el tomate /**62**/15
la tómbola /**23**/21
el toque derecho /**47**/13
el toque izquierdo /**47**/17
torcer /**66**/10
torcido /**74**/5a
el tornillo de rosca /**25**/9
el torno /**42**/16
el toro /**36**/23
la toronja /**61**/30
el torpedero /**48**/12
el torpedo /**45**/17
la tortuga /**59**/2
la torre /**52**/4
la torre de conducción eléctrica /**37**/5
la torre de control /**44**/20
la torre de enfriamiento /**37**/8
el tractor /**36**/18
el traje /**11**/6; **13**/5, 10

el traje de baño /**35**/20
el traje de judo /**46**/23
el traje espacial /**4**/21
el traje pantalón /**13**/2
el tramo /**72**/5
el tramo de escaleras /**72**/5
el transatlántico /**43**/20
el transbordador /**43**/15
la transparencia /**52**/30
el transportador /**18**/12
el trapo /**31**/7
la tráquea /**9**/22
el traspalador /**23**/17
el travesaño /**40**/15
el tren /**41**/1
Los Triángulos /**68**
la tribuna de los testigos /**16**/18
el trigo /**36**/14; **63**/2
el trípode /**19**/13; **52**/28
triste /**74**/11b
el trombón /**49**/20
la trompa /**57**/22
la trompeta /**49**/19
el tronco /**27**/12; **63**/12
el Trópico de Cancer /**5**/3
el Trópico de Capricornio /**5**/5
la trusa /**35**/20
la tubería /**37**/12
el tubo /**73**/13
el tubo de dentrífico /**73**/13
el tubo de ensayo /**19**/22
el tubo de escape /**38**/7; **40**/35
el tubo de gorna /**19**/14
el tubo de respiración /**35**/16
la tuerca /**25**/13
el tulipán /**62**/22
la turbina /**44**/16

ultimo /**75**/10b
la uña /**8**/31
el uniforme /**16**/3
universo /**4**
las uvas /**61**/12

la vaca /**36**/21
vacío /**74**/8a
el vagón /**41**/4
el vagón de carga /**41**/28
la vaina /**62**/4
la valija /**67**/19
la válvula /**40**/13; **49**/2
el valle /**34**/6
la vara corredora /**49**/21
el vaso /**30**/36; **33**/18; **73**/4
el vaso de papel /**67**/8
el vaso de precipitación /**19**/15
el vaso de vino /**51**/27
los vegetales /**20**/18
la vejiga /**9**/28
la vela /**43**/2
el velocímetro /**38**/16
la vena /**9**/29
la venda /**17**/27
el vendaje /**17**/27
el vendedor /**55**/9
el vendedor de frutas /**55**/1
la ventana /**26**/8
la ventanilla de boletos /**41**/14
los Verbos /**64**; **65**; **66**
las verduras /**20**/18
la vereda /**27**/18; **34**/17
el vestíbulo /**28**
el vestido /**13**/10
La Vestimienta /**10**; **11**; **12**; **13**
la vía /**41**/24
el viaducto /**39**/2
la vía férrea /**41**/24
Viaje /**43**; **44**
Viaje Aéreo /**44**